How to Discipline Kids without Losing Their Love and Respect

An Introduction to Love and Logic

How to Discipline Kids without Losing Their Love and Respect

An Introduction to Love and Logic

The Love and Logic
PRESS Inc.

The Love and Logic Press, Inc.

2207 Jackson Street

Golden, CO 80401-2300

www.loveandlogic.com

800-338-4065

Library of Congress Cataloging-in-Publication Data

Fay, Jim.
  How to discipline kids without losing their love and respect : an introduction to love and logic / Jim Fay.-- 1st ed.
     p. cm. 4238 2936 ⅟₁₀
  ISBN 1-930429-48-7
  1. Discipline of children. 2. Parenting. 3. Parent and child. I. Title.
  HQ770.4.F39 2004
  649'.64--dc22
                    2003027175

Project Coordinator: Carol Thomas

Editing by Jason Cook, Denver, CO

Cover design by Michael Snell, Shade of the Cottonwood, Topeka, KS

Interior design by Michael Snell, Shade of the Cottonwood, Topeka, KS

F OR OVER FIFTY YEARS, Jim Fay has worked with schools, families, and children in the areas of teaching, parenting, and discipline. In 1978, along with internationally renowned psychiatrist Foster W. Cline, he founded the Love and Logic Institute. Since that time, Love and Logic has been dedicated to developing easy-to-learn techniques for creating respectful and responsible kids—techniques that change lives!

In the following pages you will meet Jim Fay, a beloved father, grandfather, storyteller, and parenting expert. This book speaks to parents, educators, and community leaders about how to help kids develop responsibility and strong character while gaining their utmost love or respect.

Imagine…
Kids who are fun to be around.
Imagine…
Kids who listen the first time.
Imagine…
No more arguing.
Imagine…
Stress-free parenting and teaching!

As one of the founders of Love and Logic, I am in an extraordinary situation. I get to work with my son, Charles Fay, Ph.D. It is a rare father who gets to experience the joy of working side by side with a son who has become his best friend and personal consultant.

Charles came to our organization eight years ago, telling me, "I watched you and your friend, Foster Cline, share the joys of your friendship and teaching. I watched your enthusiasm as your first books and training programs became realities. I came to realize that what you did was not work. It was play. It was passion. It was never a job.

"I watched you and Mom setting up the business. You worked together at the dining room table, licking stamps, making flyers, helping parents and teachers on the phone, counting advertising pieces, and stapling books. Even that wasn't a job for you. It was passion. I decided that when I grew up I was going to be part of your dream to make Love and Logic a household word."

Although Charles was not part of the original presentation for Georgia Public Broadcasting from which this book was taken, we have included some of his articles about parenting. As you read them you will get a taste of his wisdom and his exceptional writing skill.

Experiment with the techniques he offers. And while you profit from his ideas, share my pride that he is an important part of the Love and Logic organization.

Thank you.

Jim Fay
President and Co-Founder
Love and Logic Institute, Inc.

TABLE OF CONTENTS

Foreword ix

ONE: Just Two Simple Rules 1

TWO: Taking Good Care of Yourself by
Setting Enforceable Limits 5

THREE: When Kids Argue About the Limits We Set 11

FOUR: Love and Logic's "Strategic Training Session" 19

FIVE: The Second Rule of Love and Logic:
How to Hand the Problem Back Instead of
Losing Your Cool 27

SIX: Creating Kids with Character 33

SEVEN: More Thoughts on the Power of Empathy 41

EIGHT: Love and Logic Even Works on Adults! 49

NINE: Additional Stories That Teach 55

KINDERGARTEN TEACHERS CAN SPOT THEM:
Kids with an Advantage in School and Life! 55

KEEP TEENAGERS SAFE BEHIND THE WHEEL
Practical Tips for Parents Who Want to Be Sure 60

THE EVOLUTION OF THE HELICOPTER PARENT
The Turbo-Attack Helicopter Model 61

ENDING BACKTALK AND BAD ATTITUDES
Commonsense Tips for Raising Respectful Kids 65

MAKE IT MOM'S DAY ALL YEAR ROUND
*Teach Kids How to Treat Mom with the
Respect She Deserves* 66

NO MORE HOMEWORK BATTLES
*Six Tips for Helping Kids Fall in Love
with Learning* 68

TEACH YOUR KIDS TO HANDLE LIFE'S CONFLICTS
*Why It Can Be Good for Kids to See
Their Parents Disagree* 70

"TEASEPROOF" YOUR KIDS 71

THE IMPORTANCE OF CHORES 75

FOREWORD

One August evening while driving home during a typical Atlanta rush hour, a news alert came over the radio announcing there had been a fatal car crash involving a teenage driver. This was the third deadly accident involving teenagers I had heard about since the school year began. The reporter went on to explain, "...the victims were less than a mile from their high school when the sixteen-year-old driver apparently lost control of the BMW he was driving and ran off the road, killing one of the passengers."

I was overcome with a feeling of helplessness. This could be my child some day. What could I do to help prevent this from happening to my family? How could I help other families avert a similar tragedy? At that moment I was reminded of an audio my father gave me when I began my own pilgrimage into parenthood: *Four Steps to Responsibility*. The speaker on the tape was a gentleman named Jim Fay. He spoke of a situation in his own life not unlike the one facing the parents of the deceased teenager. Except in this case, his son Charles made a decision not to ride with a friend to a party one evening even though it was the only way he could get there. Charles's decision to stay home while his friends went out for a night on the town was ultimately a life-changing decision. The life of the friend who offered the ride, as well as the lives of all the other occupants of the vehicle, were tragically cut short later that evening.

As I thought about all I had just heard on the radio, I realized that of the three recent accidents none of the drivers had been a long way from home or in a mechanically compromised vehicle. To the contrary, they were very close to home, *and* they were driving brand new cars—nice cars.

I arrived home with a question still in my mind: How did Charles, who was only sixteen at the time, make such a mature decision? How can I help myself and other parents raise more responsible kids? I searched for the audio my father had given me. Upon finding it, I ran back to my car, popped it in the player, and took a long drive. I returned home later that evening a different person. I had a mission. Every parent must know about Love and Logic. I called the 800 phone number printed on the back cover of the audio box fully expecting to leave a voice message for a customer service representative who might call me back in a few days. I was startled when a live human being answered the phone. I must have sounded quite amusing. "Uh, yes… I'm a television producer in Atlanta and, umm…I want to know more about this Jim Fay person. Could I…? Could you…?" I stammered.

"Would you like me to have Jim call you?" the nice young lady asked. "He is out of town, but I know he would love to speak with you."

"That would be great, thanks," I replied. And Jim did call me the very next day.

Over the ensuing months, Jim and I discussed many ideas by phone about how to create a television show around the Love and Logic philosophy. On one occasion, I flew to Chicago to see one of his seminars. While seated in a large, crowded hotel conference room, I observed hundreds of parents and teachers taking notes, laughing, and staying totally engaged in Jim's message. I realized all I needed to make a great television show was to re-create the experience of being at a Love and Logic seminar. The result was an entertaining hour of Jim's stories and life lessons upon which this book is based.

While I was working on this project, world-changing events have transpired (most notably, 9-11). This day turned every American's heart and mind toward home, and my heart was no exception. I became more focused on my family, and thanks to Jim Fay, learned a great deal about being a better parent. I am a recovering "Drill Sergeant" parent. To my amazement, I have witnessed many practicing "Drill Sergeants" suddenly transmogrify into their children's "buddy" in a futile effort to win their love. The results were disastrous. So the question is: How do we discipline our kids without losing their love and respect?

We all want the best for our children and I am convinced that most parents are doing the best they know how. But in an effort to do our best, we often miss the mark. The pervasive attitude, "I want my kids to have more than I had when I was growing up," is crippling, *not* enabling or empowering. What kind of message are we sending our kids when we buy a new car for their sixteenth birthday—responsibility or entitlement? How can we save the lives of our children? It is not through legislation; it is through education.

The practice of making decisions is exactly that. Practice. Practice early and practice often is the advice you will hear from Jim Fay. This was the case with his son Charles. He was allowed to practice making decisions at a young age, and as a result, he became a very responsible teenager capable of making a life-or-death decision. To quote Jim Fay, "…let our kids make decisions and mistakes while the price tag is still affordable."

I have heard it said: "Kids don't come with an owner's manual." Well, I believe Love and Logic is as close as you can get. It is the support system parents have been searching for all this time.

Please join me in spreading the good news. I hope you enjoy this book.

Tom Spencer
Producer / Director
Georgia Public Broadcasting
Love and Logic parent

CHAPTER ONE

Just Two Simple Rules

Are you ready to have some fun? Are you ready to laugh a little bit? Are you ready to learn some techniques that will let you say, "Come on kid, make my day"? Would it feel good to know that creating really great kids can actually be fun *and* simple? You're going to like Love and Logic. It's easy to learn. There are just two rules!

Why are there only two rules? Because raising kids is tough enough. Most parents and educators agree that it's not so easy to remember much of anything when you are in the trenches with challenging kids.

Would you agree that kids need loving limits? Would you agree that kids actually want these limits?

Our job is to set limits with kids. Many children see it as their job to test these limits. Why do they test them? Is it because they don't want them, or is it because they need the security of knowing that the limits we set are solid?

Kids want and need the security of firm, loving limits! That's the bottom line.

Can we agree that kids also need to be held accountable when they test or break limits?

How many parents and educators give in when their kids test limits or break them—even though they know that children need limits and accountability? Do you know anybody like that? Is it possible that many give in because they don't want kids to see them as being mean? Might these adults say to themselves, "I don't want to lose this kid's love and respect"?

Is that a legitimate concern? You bet!

All of our research shows that if we discipline in a way that leaves a child seeing us as mean, the child fails to learn respect, responsibility, and self-discipline.

What if I could show you how to set limits and hold kids accountable for their decisions without losing their love and respect—*and* without them seeing you as mean? Would that change your life? That's what Love and Logic is all about. That's the Love and Logic secret.

As I mentioned, Love and Logic comes down to two simple rules. What's the first?

THE FIRST RULE OF LOVE AND LOGIC:
Adults take good care of themselves by setting limits without anger, lectures, threats, or repeated warnings.

Good parents and teachers take really good care of themselves in a loving way. This means without being selfish. When we do, we model healthy behavior for kids.

Do you want your kids to grow up knowing how to take good care of themselves? Then ask yourself, "How do they learn this?" Are they going to learn this by seeing the neighbor doing it? Will they learn it best by seeing some fourteen-year-old doing it? Or would it be better if they learned it from seeing their parents and teachers doing it? Parents and teachers show children how to take care of themselves by modeling it. They model it by setting fair and loving limits.

What's the second rule of Love and Logic?

THE SECOND RULE OF LOVE AND LOGIC:
When a child causes a problem, the adult hands it back in loving ways.

The best way to think about the second rule is to imagine your kids ten or twenty-five years from now. Are they adults who make good decisions and as a result have happy lives? Or are they ill prepared for success because you solved all of their problems for them and didn't hold them accountable for their poor decisions? Love and Logic parents and teachers learn how to hold their youngsters accountable for the problems they create in ways that actually increase the love and respect their kids feel for them.

THE RULES OF LOVE AND LOGIC

Rule #1
Adults set firm limits in loving ways without anger, lecture, threats, or repeated warnings.

• Adults set limits that can be enforced without power struggles.
• Adults resist the temptation to "nag."

Rule #2
When a child causes a problem, the adult hands it back in loving ways.

• The adult holds the child accountable for solving his/her problems in a way that does not make a problem for others.

• The adult's empathy is "locked in" before consequences are delivered.

CHAPTER TWO

Taking Good Care of Yourself by Setting Enforceable Limits

As you already know, children need firm limits. Limits are the foundation of security. Children lucky enough to have limits placed on them in loving ways are secure enough to develop self-confidence. These children are easier to teach, spend less time acting out, and usually get along well with other children and adults.

I have seen many children misbehave in a variety of ways, in a desperate attempt to get their parents to set limits. It is almost as if they were trying to say, "Don't you love me? How bad do I have to act before you will set some limits for me?"

Setting firm limits is a gift of love. The problem is that we often find setting limits difficult. Children fight the limits to see if they are firm enough to provide security. They test us by saying that we are mean or that we don't love them. It is easy to become confused at this point and change the limits. That is the last thing children really need.

However, one has to remember that it is important to avoid giving orders. Orders do not set limits; they encourage battles. Consider the following order: "I've called you to dinner three times already! You get in here and eat your dinner!" It encourages the child to be late just to test the limits.

Try instead, "I'm serving dinner in five minutes. Hope you will join us. If not, breakfast will be at the regular time." This leaves the youngster with much more to think about, such as, "It doesn't sound as if Mom is going to be serving a special meal for me if I'm late."

Most parents are pleasantly surprised at the results when they describe what they plan to do, instead of telling the child what to do.

Fighting Words vs. Thinking Words

Avoid orders: "You're not going to talk to me like that in my own house!" *fighting words*

Try stating what you are willing to do: "I'd be willing to listen to you about that when your voice is as soft as mine." *thinking words*

Avoid telling what you won't do: "I'm not giving you any more allowance just because you wasted yours already!" *fighting words*

Try stating what you will do: "Don't worry sweetie. You'll have more money when your usual allowance comes on Saturday." *thinking words*

Instead of getting into a fight by saying, "Get yourself home by ten!" experiment with saying, "You may drive the family car as long you're home by ten."

Set limits using "thinking words" instead of "fighting words."

As we continue thinking about limits, let's spend more time examining the difference between an effective limit and an invitation to do battle.

Am I picking a fight when I say something to you like this: "Don't you talk to me like that! You get a civil tongue in that mouth. You show a little respect!"? Am I setting a limit or picking a fight? Which is it? I'm picking a fight and I'm creating resistance.

Would it help if I raised my voice? Would it help if I added on the phrase that all resistant kids live and die to hear us say…so they know that we are at the end of our rope and have no skills left? The phrase we use when we are in a state of desperation?

I MEAN IT!

Does that help?

All I've done is picked a fight. At the Love and Logic Institute we call this type of ineffective statement the "you will" message: "You will do what I tell you to do when I tell you to do it!" This doesn't set any limits but it may make us feel tough in the short term.

How about this one: "Hurry up! I'm tired of waiting for you. You want me to lose my job, is that it? Get yourself up here. Now!"

Did I set a limit or pick a fight? I picked a fight.

How about this one: "I spent a lot of time preparing that meal and now you're going to eat it and you're going to sit here till you do and you're not going to be feeding it to the dog. I saw that. And don't be wrapping it up in your napkin. You know there are starving kids in the world who..."

How am I doing? Once again I picked a fight!

How about: "Why are you in here begging for your allowance? I gave you your allowance already. What did you do, you wasted it? See, that's all you did. I am not an automatic teller machine for crying out loud! You know money doesn't grow on trees. And you better look at me while I'm talk to you. Don't you roll your eyeballs at me, I'll slap them right off your face. See, that's the attitude right there. I tell you and I tell you, but oh no, you never listen 'cause you know all the answers. In one ear and right out the other. If I've told you once, I've told you a thousand times. Okay, I'll give it to you this time, but this is the last time."

How is this parent doing? They're working really hard and using a lot of energy. Is this good modeling? I'm afraid not. Are they taking good care of themselves? Not at all. Are they setting a good example? No!

How can we *really* set limits? It can be simple! Experiment with describing how you are going to run your life. That's called the "I will" message or the "enforceable statement."

FIGHTING WORDS VERSUS ENFORCEABLE STATEMENTS

Fighting Words ("You will" statements)	Enforceable Statements ("I will" statements)
Please sit down. We're going to eat now.	We will eat as soon as you are seated.
Please be quiet. I can't listen to your brother when you are both talking at the same time.	I'll be glad to listen to you as soon as your brother has finished talking to me.
Clean your room so we can go shopping.	I'll be happy to take you shopping as soon as your room is clean.
I'm not going to play ball with you until all of you are quiet.	I'll be happy to play ball with you as soon as it is quiet.
You can't go play until you have finished your homework.	Feel free to go play as soon as you have finished your homework.
Don't be bothering your sister.	You are welcome to stay with us as long as you are not bothering your sister.
Keep your hands to yourself.	Feel free to stay with us when you can keep your hands to yourself.
Do your chores on time or you'll be grounded.	I'll be happy to let you go with your friends as soon as your chores are finished.
Don't talk to me in that tone of voice!	I'll listen as soon as your voice is as calm as mine.
You show some respect.	I'll be glad to discuss this when respect is shown.
Don't be late coming home from school.	I drive to practice those who arrive home on time.
I'm not picking up your dirty clothes.	I'll be glad to wash the clothes that are put in the laundry room.
I'm not loaning you any more money.	I loan money to those who have collateral.
You're not going out without your coat.	You may go out as soon as you have your coat.

MORE EXAMPLES OF ENFORCEABLE STATEMENTS

- I charge two dollars a minute for listening to bickering in the back seat.
- Breakfast is served for the next fifteen minutes. Get what you need to hold you until lunch.
- I give treats to kids who protect their teeth by brushing.
- I'll listen when your voice is calm.
- I love you too much to argue.
- I allow kids to drive the family car when they have made a deposit into my savings account equal to the insurance deductible.
- I allow kids to drive my car when I don't have to worry about alcohol.
- The car is leaving in ten minutes. Will you be going with your clothes on your body or your clothes in a bag?
- I'll be happy to do the things I do for you around here when I'm feeling respected and the chores are done.
- I'm going to do something about this.
- I will love you regardless of how hard or how happy you make your own life.
- I will love you regardless of the number of years it takes you to pass the seventh grade.
- I will help you with your homework as long as I can see that you are working harder than I am.
- The bus comes at about 7:45. Will you be riding it for free or paying someone to take you?
- I report illegal activities to the police.
- I buy clothes that I feel good about.
- I keep the toys I pick up.

CHAPTER THREE

When Kids Argue
About the Limits We Set

Kids have many creative ways of pushing our "buttons" to see if we love them enough to stick with the limits we set. Let's start with kids who roll their eyes. Would you like a little technique for that? This one was taught to us by a great teacher in Colorado. I watched her handle a female student who was trying to push her buttons by rolling her eyeballs. How did this teacher handle it? She looked at the student with a little bit of astonishment. Then she asked, "Can you see your brains when you do that?"

Wouldn't it be fun to be able to pull that one off? I bet you can't wait for the next time a kid rolls their eyes so that you can give that technique a shot!

There's another trick for handling kids who like to roll their eyeballs, drop their chins, and say "Whatever."

Experiment by saying the following: "Sweetie, I wanted to tell you something, but today I thought it would be kind of fun if you rolled your eyes while I did it. Could you do that? Now don't wait until I get through. Go ahead and roll your eyes while I'm talking."

What happens when we tell a really stubborn kid to do something? It becomes kind of hard for them to do it. That's like saying to a kid, "Now you get yourself to your room, and I want you to stomp your feet all the way down that hall. When you get to your room, I want you to slam that door. If you don't slam it good enough the first time, you keep slamming that sucker until you get it right."

Now what's this kid going to think? "Wait a minute, you can't tell me what to do. I'm not gonna stomp my feet and I'm sure not gonna slam that door!"

What happens if the kid does it anyway? At least we can say to ourselves, "Wow, look at that, she finally did what I asked her to do!"

Let's take a look at a fairly common situation…and how a strong-willed kid will surely test limits by talking back and arguing.

How about a kid who has wasted his allowance and now wants you to give him more money? How do you effectively set a limit? By using an enforceable statement, such as, "Saturday night at six o'clock is when I give out allowance."

No strong-willed kid is going to stand up and say something like, "Oh Dad, good skill. You really, really upgraded your parenting techniques. I bet you're proud of that. You took that Love and Logic course didn't you? Wow, that's really helping!"

What is this kid really going to say when he realizes that he'll have to wait until Saturday?

"But it's not fair, it's not fair!"

If he's like many challenging kids, he'll start manipulating. In fact, many youth take this as a challenge.

Many seem to reason, "As a representative of all American youth, it's my obligation to accept this invitation to battle. I must argue, manipulate, and try to get my parent to either back down or give me an entertaining display of anger and frustration."

How do we handle this? By going "brain dead" and not giving much thought to what the kid is saying.

Why do we go brain dead when kids start to argue? If we don't, what happens? Words start coming out of our mouths and our faces start to turn red.

Have you ever noticed how kids are masters at throwing our words right back at us?

When a child says, "But it's not fair," go brain dead and repeat just one phrase. "I know" is one of the most popular Love and Logic "one-liners."

What can a kid do with those two words? He or she will get mad and will most likely say something like, "That's stupid."

What should our answer be? "I know."

Remember: Don't think at a time like this. If you do, you'll get into trouble. Just keep it simple by softly repeating the same thing.

A loving smile can also increase the power of this technique!

What will we hear from the child next?

"But I really needed that money."

And our answer should be…"I know."

"But I promised all my friends I was gonna…"

"I know."

"Now you're making a liar out of me."

"I know."

"Well next you're going to ask me to do more chores. I wasn't born into this family to be a slave."

"I know."

"I'm begging ya, I'm begging ya."

And what's our answer? "I know."

Are you starting to recognize the power of this anti-argue technique? It's easy to feel a bit smug at this point. Be careful! Don't let sarcasm creep into your voice. Sarcasm will make it all backfire!

When the child starts to realize that their tactic is not working, they will take it up a level. Their next move will likely involve some statement that rips our heart right from our body.

"Well I didn't ask to be born into this crappy family in the first place."

What's our answer? "I know."

If the child says, "Well this sucks," what's the answer?

"I know."

Is the child going to think, "Wait a minute, manipulation just does not seem to work, I'm going to have to clean up my act"? No! Most will think, "Wait a minute, Manipulation Level One did not work, I'm forced to go to level two."

What does Manipulation Level Two sound like? "You don't love me, if you loved me…"

Would you like an answer for level two?

Don't say a word, just smile, that's right, just smile.

I'm reminded of a woman who came up to me during our annual Rocky Mountain Conference about three years ago. She was so excited!

She ran up and said, "Jim, Jim, you want to see my new tattoo?"

"I don't know. Where is it?"

She smiled and said, "It's right here on my finger."

On the first joint of her first finger she'd taken a pen and drawn a little smiley face.

I asked, "What's that there for?"

She said, "When my kids say that I don't love 'em, I just whip that out and I look at it and it reminds me to grin."

But why do you grin when your kids are giving you a hard time? Because this shows them that you can handle them without breaking a sweat.

This woman also had two words on this finger. The word on the second joint was "nice" and the word on the last joint was "try." "Nice try." When her kids would say, "You don't love me," she would just whip that finger out, look at it, and say (with a big grin), "Nice try."

Can we use this "nice try" response in other situations? You bet. How about the following?

Kid: "Well, these sneakers are only $200."
You: "Nice try."
Kid: "How can I do the assignment, I forgot my book at school."
You: "Nice try."
Kid: "Jim's parents give him $50 a week for allowance."
You: "Nice try."
You: "No homework again tonight?"
Kid: "We don't have homework anymore, it's a new policy."
You: "Nice try."

"I know" or "Nice try" might not seem natural or comfortable to some parents or teachers. Listed below are some additional "one-liners" designed to neutralize arguments. Just pick one you like and repeat it like a broken record.

"Probably so."

"I bet it feels that way."

"What do you think you're going to do?"

"I don't know. What do you think?"
"Bummer. How sad."
"Thanks for sharing that."
"Don't worry about it now."
"That's an option."
"I bet that's true."
"Maybe you'll like what we have for the next meal better."
"What do you think I think about that?"
"I'm not sure how to react to that. I'll have to get back to you on it."
"I'll let you know what will work for me."
"I'll love you wherever you live."

Remember: These "one-liners" are only effective when said with genuine compassion and understanding in your voice. These are never intended to be flippant remarks that discount the feelings of the child. If an adult uses these responses to try to get the better of a child, the problem will only become worse. The adult's own attitude at these times is crucial to success.

When your kids say, "You don't love me!" do you ever have fantasies about what you'd really like to say? Aren't you glad that they're just fantasies?

What can we say when our kid comes up with, "You don't love me!"?

Experiment with the following: "I used to say the very same thing to my parents when I was your age." Then you add, "but it worked for me."

What happens when your child takes it up a notch to Manipulation Level Three?

Kid: "You're mean, I hate you."
You: "I know!" or "Nice try."

Have you ever known a kid to go to Manipulation Level Four?

Kid: "I don't have to put up with this. I'm going to go live with Dad. I'm going to go live with my friends."

Or this one:

Kid: "I'd rather live on the street than in this police state."

Would you like an answer for that? How about a loving one? My personal favorite is, "I'll love you (pause) wherever you live."

Here are a couple thoughts to ponder: Do people who use these skills have a calmer life? Do they have more energy left over at the end of the day?

Yes!

Let's review these essential skills:

STEP ONE:

When a child starts to argue, go "brain dead."

When kids are arguing, what comes out of their mouths doesn't always make much sense. When we think too hard about this nonsense, our faces tend to turn red. Lectures start to flow from our mouths. When this happens, we lose control while our kids gain it.

Do yourself a favor: The next time your child begins with the back-talk, go brain dead.

STEP TWO:

Select your favorite Love and Logic "one-liner."

While resisting the urge to provide a lengthy yet ineffective lecture, pick just one loving statement you can say to your child.

As you say your one-liner, be sure to do so in a loving yet firm manner. Yelling, "I LOVE YOU TOO MUCH TO ARGUE!" won't have the desired effect.

STEP THREE:

If the child continues to argue, repeat yourself like a broken record.

Regardless of what the child says, continue to say the very same one-liner. The louder the child gets, the softer your voice should become. For example:

Kid: "My friends get to watch rated 'R' movies."

You: "I love you too much to argue."
Kid: "But…why are you so old-fashioned?"
You: "I love you too much to argue."
Kid: "If you loved me, you'd let me watch!"
You: "I love you too much to argue."

STEP FOUR:
Walk away.
It is much harder for a child to have a successful argument with an adult when the adult is not there. Joking aside, wise parents and teachers turn around and put some space between themselves and the angry child. Some parents lock themselves in the bathroom. Others step outside on the porch. Others call a friend who'll watch the kids—and charge the kids for the baby-sitting!

For over twenty-five years, thousands of parents and teachers across the country have used this method to bring the fun back into parenting and teaching. One couple noted:

"We started using 'We love you too much to argue' over ten years ago. That one sentence changed our relationship with our kids. Within a week of being consistent and using this phrase every time our kids started to argue, our oldest son said, 'Oh I know. You love me too much to argue.' Then he gave up and walked away! We couldn't believe our ears. It's amazing how seven little words changed our lives."

CHAPTER FOUR

Love and Logic's "Strategic Training Session"

Have you ever had trouble getting your kids ready to go in the morning so that you could get to work on time? That's a pretty universal problem isn't it? A woman came up to me in Evergreen, Colorado, and said, "If my kid makes me late for work one more time I'll lose my job." Then she said, "I've tried everything, nothing will work on this kid."

I asked, "If nothing is working, why are you asking me for help?"

She said, "Well I thought maybe you had an idea."

I replied, "I do, and I can guarantee that it will be fun!"

Before she could use my idea, I needed to make sure she had two basic Love and Logic skills.

The first skill was the one you learned in the previous chapter…how to put an end to arguing.

The second skill she needed was the one you read about in Chapter Two…how to set limits with enforceable statements.

After getting these two skills nailed down, we talked about a very special Love and Logic technique called the "strategic training session."

When we don't know what to do or how to handle a problem, it's time to sit back and develop a strategic training plan. Once we think our plan is ready, we don't use it. That's right, we don't use it.

First, we need to go to our friends and share our plan. We simply say, "I'm working on a plan to make sure that I get to work on time. To do this I need to make sure that Brian cooperates and gets himself ready to leave the house at 7:30." Then we share our plan and see if they can find any loopholes. The most important question we must ask is: "What might go wrong? What am I missing?"

Our friends will always be happy to tell us what is wrong with our thinking. It's helpful if we ask them to find all of the "holes" in our plan: "What happens if he does this? What if he says that? What if he throws a fit? What if, what if, what if?"

The next thing we need to do is plug the "holes." That is, we must figure out what we will do if our child tries to sabotage the plan.

Once this mother had a foolproof plan and made sure that all the holes had been plugged, it was time to put her plan into action. She went home and said to her little child, "Brian, I'm so excited. Starting tomorrow I'm going to be at work on time every single day. You know why? Because my car will be leaving at 7:30 in the morning. By leaving at 7:30 I'll have plenty of time to drop you off at school and then drive to the office."

She continued, "Now Brian, there's two ways for you to go: with your clothes on your body or with your clothes in a bag. I can't wait to see what you decide."

The first hole she needed to plug was to make sure that her nosey next-door neighbor (who had a habit of peeking out through her curtains and spying) didn't interfere. She called the neighbor and said, "Tomorrow morning at precisely 7:30 a.m. we are going to have a Love and Logic moment at our home. Here's what you can do to help…"

She proceeded to fill the nosey neighbor in on the entire plan, making sure that she stressed that Brian would not be in any danger. She knew that this was something the neighbor needed to hear. This is something that people need to be told—that our plan will in no way harm the child.

She filled the neighbor in on everything: "Here is how I'm making sure he's safe… Here is why I'm doing this… Here's what should happen next…" Then she added, "Oh, and by the way, if you peek out through your kitchen curtains, you can actually watch this happen."

The next call she made was to the Social Services office. She told them, "We're having a Love and Logic training session tomorrow morning. Here's how I'm making sure he's safe…" and she filled them in on the entire plan.

She added, "I wanted to make sure I filled you in, I didn't want it to be a surprise. I have a really nosey neighbor and I wouldn't be surprised if she called you to report this."

The next call went to the daycare center. She told them all about the plan. She finished with, "This is how you can help. If Brian appears at your door tomorrow morning with his clothes in a bag please do not let him join the rest of the kids until he gets himself dressed."

I would like to add something here:

There are basically two kinds of kids in the world. One is what I call the "Type-A Kid." This kid cannot wait to find out what you want so that he can give it to you. This child is hardwired from birth to believe that the world is a win-win place. He says to himself, "If I know what you want me to do, you'll do the same for me and everybody wins." The second type of youngster is the "Type-B Kid." This is the kid who cannot wait to hear what you want so that he can make sure you never get it. This child would rather die than give in to you.

Brian was a Type-B Kid. He lived to figure out what his mother wanted so he could do the opposite!

What will Mom do if Brian is not ready to leave for daycare at 7:30? What if he refuses to get in the car? No problem, Mom had those holes plugged too. Her next call went to Mabel, the baby-sitter. I'm a firm believer that all kids should have two types of baby-sitters. One baby-sitter is the baby-sitter from heaven. This is the baby-sitter whom all kids love. They play games together, they read books—they have a wonderful time, and the kids look forward to seeing her. The other is Mabel…the babysitter from hell. Mabel is trained to do two things: Number one is to make sure that the child is safe. Number two is to make sure that the child realizes how nice and special their parents really are.

Mabel is trained to be very business-like and pretty boring. She's not mean, but she's not too fun to be around.

Mom and Mabel came up with a great plan. Mom instructed her

to park her car out at the curb and be ready to go into action. If Brian refused to leave the house, Mabel was to come inside and baby-sit for the day. Mabel wasn't there to entertain Brian and she wasn't there to make sure that Brian had fun. She was there to make sure he was safe for the day.

What's the next question? Who will be responsible for paying for this day of baby-sitting? Since Mom would have to hire Mabel for the possibility that Brian refused to be ready to leave at 7:30, who do you think will be paying for that baby-sitter? Yep, Brian will be footing the bill. Mom explained to Mabel that Brian would need to pay with some of his toys since he didn't have any money.

What if Brian tries to pay with an old, used toy? That was not the plan. The plan called for him to pay with his latest and best toy, not some burned-out old toy he had outgrown and didn't want anymore.

Mom finally had all of the bases covered.

She went to bed that night and prayed, "Please Lord…" Did she pray for Brian to be read or not ready? NOT to be ready! Why? So that he could have a real-world learning experience! The next morning rolled around, and at 7:30 do you think Brian was ready to go? No, Brian was not ready.

Mom's prayer was answered.

Handling this just the way she had practiced, she said, "Brian, I see you're not ready to go."

Brian whined, "I don't have enough time."

Now it was time for Mom to put her plan into motion. The first thing she had to do was provide a strong dose of empathy. Mom had learned that one way to make sure that Brian learned responsibility, rather than resentment, was to lock in some genuine empathy before telling him about the consequence.

Providing empathy means that we show the child that we still love them…and that we are truly sad for them—even though they will still be receiving a consequence for their misbehavior or poor decision.

Some Benefits of Delivering Love and Logic Consequences with Empathy
• The child is not distracted by the adult's anger.
• The child must "own" their pain rather than blaming it on the adult.

- The adult–child relationship is maintained.
- The child is much less likely to seek revenge.
- The adult is seen as being able to handle problems without breaking a sweat.
- The child learns through modeling to use empathy with others.

Keep Your Empathy Short, Sweet, Simple, and Repetitive

Most adults find it difficult to deliver empathy when a child has misbehaved. The more natural tendency is to show anger, threaten, and lecture. Parents generally find it much easier to pick just one Love and Logic empathetic response to repeat over and over with their kids. When children hear this same statement repeated over and over, they learn two things:

- "My parents care about me."
- "My parents aren't going to back down: they mean business. No use in arguing!"

Pick Just One Love and Logic Empathetic Response and Use It Repeatedly

Examples:

1. "I'm so glad you are okay. This has got to be horrible for you. How are you planning to pay for the damage you did to the car?"
2. "What a bummer. I'd love to take you to the game, but you forgot to do your chores."
3. "This is so sad. I had to go to school and talk with your teacher about your behavior. What chores will you be doing to pay me for my time and the gasoline it took to drive there?"

Let's get back to Brian and his mother.

With great empathy, she said, "How sad. Well, that's why I have this nice little grocery bag. You can put your clothes in the bag and you can dress whenever you feel like it, there's no hurry."

Bag in one hand, kid in the other, Mom headed straight out the front door. And do you know that Mother Nature became part of the training team that morning? It had snowed the night before in Evergreen, Colorado. Brian was out there in his bare feet: "My feet are cold. My feet are cold."

Mom said to me (and to herself that morning), "Here's a kid who usually loves to run in the snow in his bare feet. I really have to watch him or his feet will get frostbit."

What did she say when Brian screamed, "My feet are cold!"?

With great empathy, she replied, "I know."

Brian didn't like this answer, so he upped the ante: "But my friends don't have to go to school with their clothes in a bag."

"I know," his mother repeated, as she gently put him into the car.

Did he take this lying down, or go for the jugular? From the back seat Mom heard, "If you loved me, I wouldn't be in the car in my pajamas with no shoes."

What did she say? "Nice try."

Oh, that made him so mad, so he pulled out the rest of his tricks. He was now kicking the back of her seat. He was raging. He was roaring. He was whining. He was even waving at passing motorists like he was being kidnapped. Then she heard his squeaky little voice in the back seat mumble quietly, "Guess I better be dressed and ready to go from now on."

Whose idea was it for him to be dressed and ready to go in the future? His!

Everyone at the daycare center was waiting with wild anticipation. They were all ready to say, "Good morning Brian, you're welcome to come in just as soon as you get dressed. Now take your time. There's no hurry."

Oh, the disappointment. When he arrived he was fully dressed. To this very day they stand around that daycare center and ask this, "How did that kid get dressed in the back seat of the car with his seat belt on?"

What about the rest of the people in our little scenario? What about Mabel? She never had to set foot in that house that day. She just drove home…a little disappointed, I'm sure. Then there was that nosey neighbor. I bet she was *more* than a little disappointed.

What do you think? Did Mom break the cycle of anger, frustration, begging, and pleading? And how did she set and enforce limits? It was simple. She put a strategic training session together and she plugged all of the holes. Then she described how she was going to run her life, instead of telling Brian what to do. She was never late to work again. Brian was ready to leave at 7:30 sharp every day.

Four keys to a successful Strategic Training Session

1. **Time:**
Conduct the training session only when you have plenty of time to pull it off.

2. **Energy:**
Conduct the training session only when you have the energy, feel relaxed, and it's a convenient time for you.

3. **Support:**
Conduct the training session only after you have "plugged all of the holes" in your plan by informing others, getting their ideas, and getting their cooperation.

4. **Rehearsal:**
Conduct the training session only after you have thought it through, practiced, and can no longer wait for your child to give you an opportunity to use your new skills!

I gave you an example of a mother who used the Strategic Training Session to teach her son to get ready in the morning. Are there plenty of other problems you can use this approach for? You bet!

Have you ever noticed that children have an uncanny knack for knowing when their parents are vulnerable to "kid attack"? As one mother put it, "Little Susie behaves just great when we happen to be going somewhere she wants to go, but just let it be a shopping trip for me and the kid goes wild. It always happens in a public place where I just can't seem to get control of the situation. Everybody stares at us and I'm always so embarrassed that I could just die."

The bad news is that this is something that seems to happen to all of us. Kids turn on their little radar sets and find ways to get the upper hand when we have the least amount of tactical support.

They usually sense that our minds and hands are busy, and that we want to avoid embarrassment in public. The result is that they often get by with the same misbehavior time and time again.

The good news is that once they have played their hand a few times by waging war in public, we can counter with a Strategic Training Session. This maneuver has brought warmth to the heart of many a parent, and has helped develop happier, more responsible kids.

Recently, the mother who told us about little Susie employed this approach with some outstanding results. She called her best friend, saying, "I've been having trouble with Susie at the store, and I need your help. Would you station yourself at the pay phone outside the store tomorrow at 10:30? I have a feeling you are going to get a call." They visited on the phone, set up the plan, and plugged all of the holes.

Mother and Susie went shopping the next day and Susie was her usual obnoxious self. Mom, in a quiet voice, asked Susie, "Would you rather behave or go sit in your room?" Susie called Mom's bluff and continued to act up.

The next thing Susie knew she was being escorted to a phone where Mom dialed a number then simply said, "Shopping is not fun today. Please come!"

Susie still figured this to be a ploy and continued her whining and begging. Thirty seconds later, Susie's eyes became very large as she saw Mom's best friend coming up to her saying, "Let's go to your room. You can wait for your mother there."

Susie was escorted home and sent to her room. Mother had a quiet shopping experience and Mother's best friend relaxed and watched television. Susie got to come out of her room once Mother came home. Susie appeared most happy to see her mother again. Mother was pleasant and friendly because she'd had a great time shopping all by herself.

Our victorious mother reports that she and her friend set up another Strategic Training Session the next day. Susie started her usual store behavior with squinty eyes and whining mouth. However, when she was questioned about whether she would rather shape up or go to her room, her eyes suddenly become very large and her mouth became very shut.

CHAPTER FIVE

The Second Rule of Love and Logic: How to Hand the Problem Back Instead of Losing Your Cool

The second rule of Love and Logic states: When children create problems, adults hand these problems back in loving ways.

By now, you've learned that "handing the problem back" means allowing children to experience the consequences of their actions. You've also learned that the best way to make this happen is to deliver a strong and sincere dose of empathy before you deliver the consequence.

Here's the problem: When kids do the unexpected (or the extremely upsetting), how many of us find it easy to deliver empathy and at the same time come up with an immediate, meaningful, and legal consequence?

Under these circumstances, do you typically have a strong dose of empathy on the tip of your tongue? Does a wonderful logical consequence pop into your head in a matter of seconds?

If your answer is "No!" don't feel guilty! Not many parents or teachers do.

I gave a workshop for five hundred practicing psychologists in Detroit, Michigan. I stood in front of all of these trained professionals and I asked, "How many of you are good at coming up with immediate and meaningful consequences with kids?"

No hands went up.

Finally one guy said, "Hey, we don't apologize for that. If you want to come up with consequences that are meaningful, you have to take a little time. It usually means several adults get together and brainstorm it. They think about the unique kid and the unique situation. And you take your time. It can't be immediate." He said, "We can't do that."

Although "experts" often preach that we must always deliver immediate consequences for misbehavior, there are many reasons why this isn't always such a great idea.

Immediate consequences work really well with rats, pigeons, mice, and monkeys. In real-world homes and classrooms, they typically create more problems than they solve.

Problems with Immediate Consequences:

1. Most of us have great difficulty thinking of an immediate consequence while we are in the middle of the problem.
2. We "own" the problem rather than handing it back to the child. In other words, we are forced to do more thinking than the child.
3. We are forced to react while we and the child are upset.
4. We don't have time to anticipate how the others will react to our response.
5. We don't have time to put together a reasonable plan and a support team to help us carry it out.
6. We often end up making threats we can't back up.
7. We generally fail to deliver a strong dose of empathy before providing the consequence.
8. Everyday we live in fear that our kid will do something that we won't know how to handle with an immediate consequence.

What if I could give you a technique that had the power of an immediate consequence but gave you time to think (and plan) when your kids pulled the unexpected? Would a technique like that lower your blood pressure?

The next time your kids do something upsetting, experiment with saying the following:

"I'm going to have to do something about that.
We'll talk later. Try not to worry."

The awareness of a consequence being on its way can serve as a consequence in itself—as long as you use the words, "Try not to worry."

When you do this, what happens? The child starts to imagine
what might happen, what can happen, what they are going to do,
and so on.

This technique also gives us plenty of time to get our friends to
help us figure out what to do. It also gives us time to plug the holes
and get ourselves calmed down so that we are not angry when we
deal with the problem and keep everyone's dignity intact. It helps us
be empathetic instead of angry.

Let's see how this happens on the home front. You have a daughter, Sharon. She's the love of your life and sixteen years old. Isn't this
the person for whom you'd lay down your life? That's how we feel
about our kids, right? And this daughter, whom you love so dearly,
went out for the evening. She said that she'd be home by 11:30 p.m.

You've been watching the clock since 11:30. You've been worrying,
and pacing, and fretting. At 2:14 a.m. all this worry starts turning
into anger.

In seven seconds flat, Sharon, the love of your life, is going to walk
through that front door, safe and sound. Is she going to hear all
about your undying love for her—or something else?

She walks through the door like she doesn't have a worry in the
world. Let's imagine that you go into a rage:

"Where have you been? I've been worried sick! No. Don't give me
those excuses! I've heard every excuse I want to hear. Don't you
roll your eyes at me, young lady. You're grounded! I heard that!
You can just add three weeks to that, 'cause I am sick and tired…"

Would you ever talk to you neighbor that way? No, not even if you
hated your neighbor. So why are you talking to her like that? After all,
this is your wonderful sixteen-year-old daughter—the one you love
so much.

Let's play it all over again. This time you're going to rehearse
beforehand so that you're ready. You will begin by plugging the
"holes." The first thing you'll want to do is call your friends and prac-

tice how you will handle the situation the next time it occurs. Practice with them what you are going to say when she walks through the door at 2:14 a.m.

And it does happen again. Let's imagine how you'd handle it with Love and Logic:

"Oh Sharon, I'm so glad you're okay. I was so worried about you. Now I know you told me I shouldn't worry so much. You always tell me not to worry, I know. But when you're gone and I don't know where you are or what you're doing, I just start imagining all these horrible things. I'm just so thankful you're okay. But you do look tired. You better get some rest, okay? Why don't you go to bed and we'll deal with this another time. Try not to worry about it tonight. Get some sleep."

What's Sharon going to say? "What are you going to do?"

You simply say, "You worry too much, Sharon. Give me a couple of days on this. I'm going to call up my friends and we're going to come up with something."

Now who's worried?

Now who's doing all of the thinking?

Who is awake in her bedroom now?

This time you won't rush things. Instead, you'll give yourself lots of time to call up your friends. Call a good teacher over at school that you've gotten to know and ask for some advice. Call a counselor. How about somebody at church? Maybe a neighbor who works well with kids?

After taking some time and talking with others, you finally have it all figured out. Now you can't wait to tell Sharon what the consequence is going to be. It's on the tip of you tongue, but you wait for the perfect time. Two days later, Sharon comes to you and says, "I want to go out tonight."

This is just what you've been waiting for! But you mustn't forget one very important factor. What needs to get locked in before she learns about the consequence of staying out too late? A strong and sincere dose of empathy!

Empathy opens the heart and mind to learning.
Empathy allows kids to learn from the
consequences of their actions.

You'll need to lock in that empathy nice and strong. With genuine sadness, you say, "Oh, this is a real bummer, that would be great, but what a bummer. I'm just not strong enough to worry about you tonight. You need stay home."

Is Sharon going to look at you and say the following?

"Oh, you took that new Love and Logic parenting course and it's finally really working and oh, I bet you're proud of your new skills!"

I don't think so! But this time you're ready with some anti-argue skills.

Sharon: "It's not fair."
You: "I know."
Sharon: "Yeah, but I'll never be late again."
You: "I know."
Sharon: "Yeah, but my friends don't even have to have a curfew."
You: "I know."
Sharon: "And how am I ever going to grow up if you just treat me like a baby?"
You: "I know."
Sharon: "We'll this sucks."
You: "I know."
Sharon: "If you loved me, if you loved me…"
You: "Nice try."
Sharon: "I don't have to put up with this, I'm going to go live with my friends."

What's the answer? "I'll love you (pause) wherever you live."

Congratulations! Nicely done. Now you have a skill you can use when your kid goes for your heartstrings. Now you don't have to be drained by seemingly endless arguments.

The next time your child does something inappropriate, experiment with saying, "Oh no. This is so sad. I'm going to have to do something about this! But not now, later, try not to worry about it."

The Love and Logic delayed or "anticipatory" consequence allows you time to "anticipate" whose support you might need, how the child might react, and how to make sure that you can actually follow through with a logical consequence. This Love and Logic technique also allows the child to "anticipate" or worry about a wide array of possible consequences.

Delayed consequences gain their power from a basic principle of conditioning: When one stimulus consistently predicts a second, the first stimulus gains the same emotional properties as the second. Stated simply: When "try not to worry about it" consistently predicts something the child really must worry about, "try not to worry about it" becomes a consequence in and of itself.

CHAPTER SIX

Creating Kids with Character

L et's talk about what creates character. I think the best way to do this is to share some more stories. This first story I heard while I was listening to the "Dr. Laura" show.

A mother called the show and told Dr. Laura, "My son is in eleventh grade and he admitted to me that he has skipped one of his classes six times."

The mother tells her son, "Now wait a minute, you're going to fail the course."

"No, I'm not going to fail the course," he tells her.

The mother then tells her son, "School policy says that if you have five unexcused absences you fail the class."

How does the son answer? "Oh, maybe some kids, but not me."

She says, "What do you mean?"

He says, "You know, you were in school once."

Mom is starting to catch on. She asks, "Hey, you didn't forge my name on some notes, did you?"

The kid answers, "Yeah Mom, but it's no big deal."

No big deal? Why would any kid in the world say "no big deal"? Because it *is* a big deal and they don't want their parent to treat it as a big deal! Anytime a kid says "no big deal," the parent needs to put on their parenting hat. This means the parent now has a big job to do.

Then the kid says to his mother, "Besides, now that I told you, you can't tell the teachers."

When Mom asks "Why?" he says, "Parent–child confidentiality."

Are you as amazed as I am that somebody would have to call a national talk show to ask if that's true? Is there any doubt in your mind about what needs to happen with this kid? Does he need to face the music? You bet he does! Now the parent has two choices. She could stand between him and his bad decision and not make him be responsible. That's one possibility.

Another possibility is that she can stand *beside* him and support him while he learns from this bad decision. Which one will create character? How do we do it so that he doesn't see Mom as the bad guy? Let me give you another story, and then we'll put this all together.

I recently had a call from a parent who was concerned about her teenager's behavior. After some discussion, Mom admitted the teen had stolen a credit card and purchased items through the Internet. However, mom's major concern was about her daughter lying about the purchases, not the criminal behavior itself.

Several times the mother said, "I just don't want her to have a record."

In desperation, I finally asked, "Are you saying you don't mind that she is a criminal, as long as she doesn't *look* like a criminal?"

"Well, no," she replied. "But this is going to be so hard for her. What do I do?"

After spending more than thirty years as an educator and a parent, it was clear to me that this mother needed to treat her daughter's mistake as an opportunity…a chance for her daughter to learn how to face the consequences of her choices. While it will cause some short-term pain, the long-term benefits will be a stronger, healthier sense of personal responsibility…the foundation of a solid character.

Of course, it's much easier to know what other parents should do about their misbehaving children. This mother is struggling with a trap many of us have fallen into. We love our children. When they are uncomfortable or hurting, we hurt even more. We want to protect them. It's only natural. However, our attempts to save children from the consequences of their mistakes have a great deal to do with comforting ourselves, instead of solving the problem.

This mom has fallen into another trap. She has bought into the belief that a child's self-concept is damaged when kids experience the consequences of their mistakes. Nothing could be further from reality. In fact, the opposite is true: Self-concept is reduced every time a parent excuses bad behavior.

What do both of these parents need to do? They need to allow their children to be held accountable for their poor decisions! This is how we create kids with good character. But how do we do this without being mean or feeling guilty?

The Love and Logic philosophy gives us a great solution for this dilemma. You've already learned it! Yes! There is a way of holding kids responsible for their actions without appearing mean or authoritarian: A strong dose of empathy. The power of empathy leaves kids thinking, "My parent is not the problem. My bad decision is the problem."

This heavy dose of empathy or compassion (which is provided before we lay down any punishment or logical consequences) opens their minds and hearts to learn from their mistakes rather than blaming us.

In the case of the stolen credit cards, let's see how this teenager's mom might help her daughter face the natural consequences of making illegal purchases. Mom needs to resist the temptation to react in anger, which will only make her youngster defensive.

A Heavy Dose of Empathy

Mom: "Oh sweetie, what a bummer. My heart goes out to you. What a problem. I bet you feel awful. Would it help if I went to the police with you and held your hand while you explain this?"

Daughter: "But Mom, it's not fair! Can't you just get me a lawyer?"

Hold the Line in a Loving Way

Mom: "Sweetie, I love you too much to let you pass up this opportunity to learn about how the real world works." *(Mom needs to repeat this statement for each new argument the child tries.)*

This is a sad story about a mother and a daughter who are paying a huge price. Neither of these people would be in this situation had mom started early handling the little problems and misbehaviors in this way.

Life provides a limited number of opportunities for children to build character and learn how the real world works. Make the most of them!

CHARACTER BUILDERS AND STEALERS

Builders	Stealers
Apply empathy before consequences.	Yell, lecture, and give your kids plenty of reasons to blame you for their problems.
Expect your children to work for most of the things they want.	Give your children everything they want.
Set loving limits and expect your children to behave.	Try to be best friends with your child and don't set limits.
Make discipline look easy.	Show frustration and make it look hard.
Show children that arguing and manipulation won't work.	Get sucked into arguments and power struggles.
Guide children to own and solve the problems they create.	Rescue your kids from their problems.
Avoid lectures and repeated warnings.	Use lectures and repeated warnings often.
Hold your kids accountable for dishonest behavior.	Make excuses for your kids and say things like, "It's just a phase. All kids do that."

Over the past thirty years, we've noticed three general types of parents. As you review the following, consider for yourself which parent creates kids with the greatest character.

Helicopters

Helicopter parents make a lot of noise, a lot of wind, and a lot of racket. They hover over and rescue their children whenever trouble arises. Often viewed as model parents, they sincerely believe they are preparing their children for the real world.

But Helicopter parents are actually "stealing" learning experiences from their children in the name of love. The message sent to the child is:

You are fragile and can't make it without me.

Drill Sergeants

Drill Sergeant parents also make a lot of noise, wind, and racket. Their motto is: "When I say jump, you jump!" The children of Drill Sergeants, like those of Helicopters, have never had the chance to make their own decisions and are dependent upon their parents. The message sent by Drill Sergeants is:

You can't think for yourself, so I'll do it for you.

Consultants

Consultant parents are always willing to give advice. Instead of rescuing or controlling, they allow their children to make decisions and experience life's natural consequences while providing guidance. Consultants are always willing to help children explore solutions to problems. They're always willing to describe how they would solve a problem themselves. But then they "blow out" and allow their children to make their own decision. Instead of dependency, the Consultant sends messages that create self-worth and strength in their children:

You are capable of thinking for yourself, making good decisions, and solving problems!

The following example indicates the difference in these three styles:

When a child complains about being picked on at school, the Helicopter says, "Don't worry, I'll tell the teacher to straighten that kid out for you." The Drill Sergeant commands, "You smack that kid the next time and he'll stop!" The Consultant replies, "That's really sad. Would you like to hear what some other kids have done to solve that?"

Tips for becoming a Consultant Parent:
- Provide suggestions instead of lecturing or rescuing.
- Allow your child to do more thinking than you.
- Let empathy and logical consequences do the teaching.
- Take good care of yourself in a nurturing way.

Consultant parents raise kids with the greatest character!

CHAPTER SEVEN

More Thoughts on the Power of Empathy

Here's a little story that really hit home with me. It proves that empathy works on all of us. It's also a good reminder that a little empathy goes a long way, whether we use it on kids, or adults.

I went down to my local Ace hardware store and bought the latest gizmo. I couldn't wait to see how it worked. When I got home I tried to use it—but it didn't work. I thought to myself, "Oh man! I couldn't wait to use this thing! Now it won't even work."

I'm so frustrated that all I want to do is go back to the store and tell the clerk and demand to know just what he's going to do about it!

Before I go any further with this story, we should talk about the brain and how it functions. There are several parts of the brain, one of them being the frontal cortex. This is where thinking takes place. Another part of the brain is the brain stem. This is where the "fight or flight" response lives. That's our defensive mode. We also have a little switch somewhere in the brain that reacts to stimuli. This switch's job is to focus brain energy either into the frontal cortex or the brain stem, depending on the need at that time.

This little "brain switch" is a threat receptor. When it activates the brain stem, what happens to the thinking process? It shuts down. This is so we can either fight quicker or flee quicker.

Now back to my story.

There I was with this great gizmo that didn't work. My frustration level was pretty high. Not only did it not work but I had to waste more time to return it.

When I go back to the store and say, "This gizmo does not work," which part of my brain will get activated if the clerk says the following?

"Of course it didn't work, I bet you didn't read the instructions, did you? See, that's what you guys do all the time. You take this stuff home and you start messing with it before you take time to read the instructions. Then it gets all messed up. Then you come in here thinking that you can just return it. Well you know what? I get sick and tired of this and…"

What part of my brain would be operational? A clerk behaving this way would surely turn me into a brain stem. And how long would it be before I said something that turned the clerk into a brain stem, too? What would we have then? We'd be stuck with two walking, talking brain stems trying to solve a problem. Not good!

Would I ever shop at this store again? Do you think I'd tell all of my friends, neighbors, and anyone who'd listen? You bet. I'd tell everyone not to shop there!

Has something like this ever happened to you? Has it ever happened in your home? Has it ever happened in your classroom? How much does it take to get the average person into brain stem mode?

Will a little criticism do it?

How about some threats?

Will a lecture or two do the trick?

How about some anger on our part?

All of the above put others into brain stem, fighting mode!

Now let's go back and play it all over again, because in reality I was dealing with a highly skilled clerk. I think he'd been to customer-service training.

I went into the store and said, "This gizmo does not work!"

With care and sincerity, he responded, "Oh, that's never good."

What part of my brain got activated? It's the frontal cortex—the thinking mode.

The clerk took the gizmo, apologized for my inconvenience, and offered to refund my money. Now he has a customer for life. And whenever I go to that store, you can guess what clerk I'm looking for. Do you think I'll ever shop at this store again? You bet I will! Do you think I'll tell all of my friends and neighbors about this store? You bet. I'll tell everyone how great that store is. I'll make sure to spread the good word.

There's another part of the brain that stays alert and active all the time. Do you know what part that is? It's the part that controls revenge and getting even. I saw it operating one day… years ago… in Denver's old Stapleton airport. I was standing behind a guy who was so outrageously nasty that I was actually embarrassed for him. It was a really snowy day and the airport had to shut down. No planes were flying. I guess this guy thought that if he was nasty enough the skies would clear and planes would suddenly be allowed to take off and land. He even got upset when the ticket agent said, "Look, if you can find another plane that's flying today we'll honor the ticket." He just kept ranting and raving at the poor ticket agent.

When it was finally my turn, I said to the agent, "Oh, that was rough." She replied, "Tell me about it."

I continued, "He had no business talking to you like that."

She agreed, "I know, but that's what happens here."

Impressed by her professionalism, I said, "Oh, but I was proud of you."

She looked at me rather shocked and said, "What?"

Once again I said, "I was really proud of you. You stayed so calm. I really don't know how you did that."

Looking very surprised, she asked, "Did I look calm?"

She continued, "I wasn't calm. I was so upset I couldn't think. In fact, I'm afraid that I might have sent his luggage to the wrong city."

Wow! Do you want to keep other people in brain stem or frontal cortex mode? Does it make sense that if we can provide empathy, instead of anger or criticism, we might just have happier lives?

For example, let's take Dick. He's in high school and is a pretty tough kid who is always in trouble. He got into a fight and needs to be kicked out of school for a few days. How should this situation be handled? Let's look at how two different types of school principals might handle this problem.

The first principal is going to set himself up to be the source of Dick's problem. Dick will hate him and fantasize about revenge.

The second is going to let Dick be the source of his own problem. This will leave Dick feeling more remorseful than revengeful.

Here's the first principal:

"Okay Dick, you know better than that! You know there is no fighting allowed here! That is a school policy and each student got a copy of the policy to take home and read. I know you took that policy home and read it because I have a copy of it right here in my hand with your father's signature on it. I have it right here in my hand!

"So you know the rules, you know how this works, and you knew it before you fought with that kid. Three days, Dick, fighting is a three-day suspension. You're out of here until Friday and don't you come back before then. And I mean it! Now get out of school and I don't want to see your face here for three days."

What's happening to the door as Dick leaves the office? Slam! That door is slammed so hard that it's hard to believe it's still on the hinges. And what happens to any kids who are unlucky enough to be in the hall as Dick is leaving school? Dick gives them a push. What about the lockers as he goes down the hall? You can bet that they will get some interesting words spray-painted on them tonight.

Did this bring the worst out of Dick? And who is Dick blaming? He is thinking, "That principal is such a jerk. Who does he think he is, kicking me out for three days? I hate school anyway. The only reason I'm here is because I gotta be here. It's the law. I hate that guy, I'll show him."

Now let's try it again, but this time with a Love and Logic principal. Shaking Dick's hand, he laments:

"Oh boy, that guy must have really irritated you. Oh man, he really got under your skin, didn't he? This is such a bummer, Dick. There's a price to pay for everything isn't there? What's the price you decided to pay to show him that he couldn't mess with you anymore? Three days' suspension, yeah you got it. So I guess we'll get to see you when? Friday. We'll look forward to seeing you back at school on Friday pal, see ya."

Is Dick still out of school? You bet. But he's acting differently about it this time.

How is he leaving the office? Is he hitting kids? Is he looking for some kind of revenge?

No, but he is confused.

He can't blame the principal. The principal was too nice to him. In fact, the principal sounded like he was looking forward to seeing him back in school. How is Dick feeling? He's actually looking forward to returning to school because this principal makes him feel wanted.

Now wait, was that the same kid? How could he react so differently to the same situation? How could one person bring the worst out of him and another bring out the best? How could one person put him into fight-or-flight while another put him into the thinking mode? Which principal really made Dick take responsibility for his actions?

For years, we wondered why two different parents could lay down the same punishment yet have such different results. One parent would be seen by the child as the source of their problem, whereas the other parent would not. We also wondered how this applied to educators. As we looked into it, we discovered that the people who were able to get children to see themselves as the source of their problem always provided sincere empathy before they described any consequence there were about to deliver. The empathy always came *before* the consequence.

Do you have an empathetic response on the tip of your tongue when your kid does something really upsetting? Most people don't.

For over twenty years, I've studied people who've learned how to replace anger with empathy. What did I find? They all had the same characteristic: they all had very limited vocabularies when it came to disciplining. They used very, very few words. In fact, the people who seemed to be able to start with empathy and do it consistently had only one empathetic response…a response that was unique to them, felt comfortable, and didn't sound phony. They kept it on the tip of their tongue and they used it every single time they had to discipline their kids. The response they used depended on their unique culture, where they lived, etc.

During my studies, I found many people who followed this very effective approach. One woman would simply say, "Oh, oh" in a sad tone of voice. That was her simple empathetic response. How much energy do you need to use that one? Does that put a person into frontal cortex mode?

I've met other people who said things like, "How sad" or "What a bummer." While these are quite different responses, both can provide a strong message of empathy if delivered with sincerity.

We met a guy who ran a boys ranch in Nebraska. No matter when we'd see him, he'd always have his cowboy duds on: boots, hat, and a shiny belt buckle with a steer on it. When any of the kids needed to talk to him about something they'd done wrong, he'd scuff one of his boots back and forth in the dust while sadly saying, "Dang."

Will that do it? Will "dang" put a kid into frontal cortex mode? Said with sincere sadness, it sure can!

Listed below are just a few of the empathetic statements we've seen people memorize and use:

- "Bless your heart."
- "That's sad."
- "Oh. That's never good."
- "Oh, honey."
- "This stinks."
- "How sad."
- "What a bummer."

Here's a way you can get that empathetic response ready to use and keep on the tip of your tongue. First, get three sets of Post-It notes and write your one empathetic response on every single one. "What a bummer." "What a bummer." "What a bummer." "What a bummer." "What a bummer."

Second, post them around your classroom or house. When you open up the cupboard, there it is, "What a bummer." When you pull out a drawer, inside it says, "What a bummer." When you look in the mirror, there it is, "What a bummer." When you lift up the toilet seat, you're reminded, "What a bummer." You get into your car and once again you say, "What a bummer."

Run some quick experiments to find out for yourself how powerful empathy really is. Can it change your life? You bet!

CHAPTER EIGHT

Love and Logic Even Works on Adults!

Is Love and Logic limited to any special age, culture, ethnicity, etc.? Could it even work on me? You bet it could. And it has! Shirley, my wife, uses this stuff on me. She's really good at it too, and I have to admit that I hate it sometimes.

Years ago she said, "Jim, would it be reasonable to ask that you get the outside of the house painted by the first of June?"

It was November, so I said, "Oh sure. No sweat. I can do that."

She continued, "I know you prefer to do it yourself because we had that bad experience with the house painter the last time. Is that enough time to get it done?"

A bit annoyed, I answered, "Oh yeah...yeah."

Then she added, "Do you want me to remind you?"

I don't like to be reminded, so I said, "No, it just makes me mad when you remind me. I'll remember. I don't need a reminder."

"Fine," she said. She kept her promise not to remind me. How nice!

Months flew by as they tend to. The first of June came and went. I'd forgotten to paint the house. On the fifteenth of June, I tried to drive into my driveway. There was a painting contractor's truck blocking it. There were ladders everywhere and people scraping and painting my house. I went into the house and asked Shirley what was happening. Very sweetly, she said, "Well, you said you could get it painted by the first of June."

Interrupting her, I blurted, "But I forgot."

"I know," she said.

"How are we supposed to be paying for this?" I asked.

She answered, "Try not to worry about it."

I snapped, "Well, I *am* worried about it! How are we going to pay for this?"

She answered sweetly, "Well, we won't have a very good vacation this year, but at least now you don't have to worry about the house getting painted."

Thirty years later, I still remember the lesson I learned from this. In fact, all Shirley has to say is, "Would it be reasonable to ask…?" and I get the message. The image of those painters and their ladders comes right back to me. And I know that she'll keep her promise not to nag or remind me. "Would it be reasonable?" sends shivers up my spine.

Shirley isn't the only one who's taught me a lesson with Love and Logic.

I've been speaking and doing seminars since 1977. There was a time in my life when I had more get-up-and-go than I have now, and I was known to give three different speeches in three different cities on the same day. I would often overextend myself and have to somehow make good on my promises. I would go to my first engagement, stand in front of the group and talk, drive like crazy to the next presentation, and so on. I often found myself standing on the side of the highway, explaining to police officers why I had to drive like crazy.

It wasn't easy to explain to the officers that I had just left a seminar where I was speaking to parents and educators about raising responsible kids and the importance of kids facing the consequences of their bad decisions. And there I was, an adult who was overextending myself (bad decision), who was driving like a fool (another bad decision), and who really didn't want to face the consequences of those bad decisions.

It soon became apparent that I needed to make some changes in my life. Somehow I needed to stop getting those tickets. You would think that the obvious solution would be that I stop overextending myself—stop trying to do so many talks in one day. Or, if I was going to keep doing so many talks, that they be close enough to each other that I could get to them on time.

I decided to go to my friend and great psychiatrist Dr. Foster Cline to see if he had any suggestions. If anyone would know, Foster would. We talked about personalities and how they match up to jobs. Do people in different walks of life have different views of life? Does a psychologist have a little different view of life than, say, an engineer? Does an engineer have a different view of life than a lawyer? Does a lawyer have a different view of life than a social worker? Yes. And what about police officers, what is their typical view of life?

Based on our conversation, I came up with a wonderful technique. By the way, please do not try this. In fact, I'm not going to give you all the components of the process.

I will tell you just one thing: When I get stopped now, I come across like the most absentminded old dude you've ever seen—thankful I'm being stopped. So thankful because, otherwise, I could probably hurt myself or someone else.

It was working! I had eleven warning tickets in a row in the state of Colorado. I was really on a roll, and I was pretty proud of that record. I had it down to a science.

And then it happened. My wife Shirley and I decided to take a trip to Florida to visit our kids. I made a horrible mistake. I exceeded the speed limit in that great state of Texas, where it seems that the police officers are trained differently.

It was during this trip that a Texas state trooper put my own moves on me before I could put them on him. He made mincemeat out of me—right out there on the side of the highway. He was so good that I didn't even know what hit me.

He got out of his patrol car with a big grin on his face and a big cowboy hat on his head. "Hey there buddy, see ya got a Colorada license plate. I bet you're on a trip. Where ya headed?"

I tried to apply my technique, "Well officer, my wife and I are headed down to Florida. Our kids live there and we haven't seen them in quite a while."

He said, "Oh, well then that explains it. I bet you're anxious to get there, huh?"

Caught off guard, I answered, "Uh, yeah, we are kind of anxious to get there. Why?"

He answered again, "Well I'll tell ya why I stopped ya… This is such a bummer."

(This is such a bummer? Wait! That's one of my lines.)

He continued, "The radar shows that you were going 73 miles-an-hour. Now that wouldn't be all that bad but this is a 55-mile-an-hour speed limit and when it gets that bad I gotta write ya'll a ticket. Now don't feel bad. Now I don't want you to worry…"

(Don't worry? I recognize that one too!)

He kept smiling as he said, "You don't have to go back to the county seat and deal with that, I know you were fret'n about that, I know you're want'n to get to those kids and we don't want to make ya backtrack. The state gives me this letter that I get to give to ya. Look at this, it'll outline all the choices you have in this matter. Look at that first choice right there, back to Berman, it's about fifteen miles, you pay the fine and it's over with. Y'all never have to think about it again."

(Oh no! Now he's giving me choices.)

Then he started to sound like a school counselor: "But I'm wondering if the second one might be a little better for ya, because I know you're anxious to see your kids, and you surely don't want to go back." Then he said, "Now you just try not to worry about this for a couple of weeks."

(Try not to worry?)

Again he said, "Just put it out of your mind."

(Oh no!)

He continued, "Sometime when you have a little time on your hands, read through this here little box and match up the speed with the dollar amount for each mile-an-hour over the limit and then you know how much money to send us. And look at all the choices they provide there, see they are right there, all the choices. Let's see, yep, ya see right here it says they will accept certified checks, cashier checks, money orders, and cash, it's really up to you. You know there's a third choice. A lot of people feel they need to contest these tickets. So on the backside…well look there…they've even outlined all the steps in contesting the ticket if you choose. See they got step one, and there's step two…ya'll might want to think a lot about that before you do anything."

Then he laid a little more empathy on me before he left: "Sure understand a car like this one getting away from ya in these long stretches of highways. These big powerful cars and these long straight Texas roads, they'll get ya every time. Now ya'll have a good trip. And ya'll come back and see us soon, ya hear?"

As I was heading back to my car, I said to myself, "I trained that guy." Getting back in the car, I complained to Shirley, "I can't believe what I just did out there! Shirley! Guess what I just did? Can you believe I just got through thanking him for the crummy ticket? Yep, that's what I did!"

This guy had my head whirling. As he talked, I kept saying to myself:

> "Am I going back to…Bur… ? No! I don't want to do that. I'm going down to Florida. Wait a minute, maybe I can contest it. Oh you can't contest it, you deserve it. You were doing 73 miles-an-hour in a 55-mile-an-hour speed limit area. You can't contest that. I wonder if they rat on you if… I wonder if I go pay the fine if… What's going to happen to my insurance?"

That Texas state trooper was so slick that I was too busy thinking to put my moves on him. What about my respect for him? Was it still pretty high? Yeah! Would you guess he got a lot less tired and less stressed-out than some other folks in his profession? You bet! That's what I hope for you.

CHAPTER NINE

Additional Stories That Teach

I've picked some of my favorite stories and added them to this book. I think you will find these additional stories to be both helpful and entertaining. These stories were written for our quarterly journal and touch on subjects that are near and dear to the hearts of both parents and educators.

KINDERGARTEN TEACHERS CAN SPOT THEM:
Kids with an Advantage in School and Life!
by Charles Fay, Ph.D.

What are the most powerful things parents can do to help their young children begin school on a positive note and enjoy a lifetime of successful learning? Over the next year (or longer) Foster W. Cline, M.D., my father (Jim Fay), and I will be answering this question in a series of articles published in the quarterly *Love and Logic Journal*.

Kicking off this theme, let's consider the following:

- During the first week of school, how can kindergarten teachers spot the children who will thrive in their classrooms?
- What characteristics also allow these kids to enjoy success throughout the elementary, middle, and high school grades?

Thousands of teachers throughout this wonderful country tell me the same thing. Students who excel begin school knowing how to:

- Sit still for at least thirty minutes at a time.
- Avoid interrupting others' conversations.
- Use polite words such as "please" and "thank you."
- Take turns and "share"… in conversations, games, and other activities.
- Show that they are paying attention by looking at adults when adults are giving instructions.
- Follow simple directions such as "Stop," "Start," "Wait," "Line up."

Sadly, not all kids have these skills. Even sadder is the frustration, sadness, and embarrassment many feel as a result. Over and over again, we hear the same story from very caring, concerned teachers:

"I'm so worried for these little ones. I can't believe what I've been seeing over the past few years! We actually had to suspend one of my kindergarten students yesterday! It's so sad. More and more of the young kids we're seeing lack the basic skills for success in school. They don't know how to stand in line, sit, listen, take turns, and follow simple directions. It's not just the kids from broken homes and poverty. We're seeing more kids with these problems from highly educated, wealthy homes. And, I can't believe how disrespectful some of these little ones are. More and more act like defiant teenagers. When I ask them to do something for me, they put their hands on their hips and say, "No!" Some of them are even using words that would make a sailor blush! What worries me is how hard life is going to be for them."

Kindergarten teachers aren't just concerned with behavior problems. They're also seeing more youngsters who lack basic academic readiness skills—skills that serve as the building blocks for reading, writing, arithmetic, and reasoning. Kids with an advantage immediately stand out. How? Because it's clear that someone in their lives:

- Spends a lot of time reading to them.
- Talks with them constantly and enthusiastically about everyday activities, such as cooking, cleaning, shopping, driving, work, etc.
- Has them playing with blocks, sand, clay, balls, crayons, paper and scissors, dolls, toy cars without batteries, and other toys that require creativity and visual-motor coordination.
- Takes them to libraries and museums.
- Does the above instead of allowing them to sit in front of the television or some other electronic device.

Each of these activities grows the brain. That's right! Each of these simple and fun activities creates new neurological pathways (or "brain connections") that give young children a powerful and life-long advantage.

In this series of articles, we'll share plenty of practical techniques for helping young children develop skills that help them stand out as winners. A great side effect of these skills is that they make parenting fun and rewarding instead of stressful and chaotic!

Let's start with the very most important thing we can do for our kids: establish ourselves as loving authority figures in their eyes. What do I mean by "loving authority figure"? Simply put, our kids see us as being someone who cares very much for them, someone who's kind, someone who can make them do things that they really don't want to, and someone who will hold them accountable for their poor decisions without resorting to anger. When children experience this magical combination of high expectations, accountability, and lots of kindness, they feel safe and loved.

What does this have to do with success in school? Consider the following:

- Who do children see when they look at their teachers?
- Who do kids see when they look at police officers?
- Who will they see when they look at their bosses someday?
- For the rest of their lives, who will they see when they encounter any other authority figure?

Their parents! That's right. The answer to all of these questions is the same. For the rest of their lives, our children will never treat their teachers, bosses, or other authority figures better than they treat us.

The key is setting firm and enforceable limits and showing our kids that we can handle their misbehavior with meaningful consequences—without breaking a sweat. The easier we make our discipline look, the more our kids begin to reason: "Wow! Even when I act the very worst I can, my parents can handle me without getting angry and frustrated. Boy are they strong, and boy am I safe."

A mother who came to one of our conferences gave her three-year-old, Rachel, a great gift. For weeks, this sweet little child had been driving her nuts every time they went grocery shopping. She'd behave pretty well until they had to wait in the checkout line. Then the whining and screaming fits would begin. Soon, all of the other shoppers were looking her way. Soon, Mom felt like digging a hole right in the supermarket floor, crawling inside, and hiding.

How likely is it that this child will someday have problems at school if she doesn't learn how to be patient and wait in line at the grocery story with her mother? What's going to happen if she decides it's fashionable to whine at school and disobey her kindergarten teacher? How is she going to feel about herself? Will she grow up to consider herself a winner? Or will she feel pretty down about herself much of the time?

Luckily, her mother was learning a few simple yet powerful skills for teaching her little girl to listen—the first time. With a twinkle in her eye, she told me how she experimented with Love and Logic:

"I took the Love and Logic parenting course offered by my school, and I planned for days before I decided to actually do it.

"There we were, standing in a long line at the store. As usual, Rachel decided to strike at that very moment by whining, running away from me, and irritating everybody around.

"This time, I looked down at her and said, 'Uh oh! This is so sad. All of this whining is really draining my energy.' Then I kept my mouth shut until later.

"As we drove by the ice cream shop on our way home, I

looked at her in the rearview mirror and said, 'This is so sad. I was thinking about stopping for ice cream, but all of my energy got used up listening to your whining at the store. When you can behave, I'll probably have more energy to take you to Dairy Cow.'

"For the rest of the week, I kept saying, 'Oh. This is sad… I don't have enough energy' every time she wanted me to do something special for her. It broke my heart to see her so upset, but now she's starting to understand that when I ask her to behave, I really mean it."

Did Rachel thank her mother for her wise and wonderful parenting plan? Did Mom hear something like, "Mommy, I love your new skills," from the back seat of the car that day? No way! "I WANT IT! I WANT IT! ICE CREAM! ICE CREAM! ICE CREAM! ICE CREAM!" was more like it. Thankfully, the long-term results of Mom's bravery shone through the next time they stood in the checkout line:

"The next time we went to the store, Rachel started to go into meltdown mode again. I leaned over, got about an inch away from her ear, and whispered, 'Uh oh. You're starting to drain my energy again.'

"It was amazing how fast she got herself back under control. And it was great! Later that day, I had a blast eating lots of ice cream and giggling with her at Dairy Cow!"

If Mom keeps up the good work, Rachel is going to dazzle some lucky kindergarten teacher in three years. Rachel will stand out because she will know that it's important to listen the first time.

Rachel will stand out because she will already have a voice in her head that reminds her, "Make good choices, because bad ones make things really sad."

Rachel will stand out because her parents are giving her the gift of self-discipline and self-esteem.

KEEP TEENAGERS SAFE BEHIND THE WHEEL
Practical Tips for Parents Who Want to Be Sure
by Charles Fay, Ph.D.

Too many of our children are injured or killed as they drive on America's roads.

Last year more than 3,500 teenage drivers were killed and 344,000 were injured in accidents, according to the National Highway and Transportation Safety Administration.

Have you ever wondered how safe a driver your teenager really is? Take the following test to see if your child is safe behind the wheel:

My teen paid for at least half of the cost of his/her vehicle and insurance.	True	False
My teen uses my car and has made a deposit into my savings account equal to the insurance deductible.	True	False
My teen is respectful and follows the rules of our home and his/her school.	True	False
My teen handles frustrations well. He/she does not lose his/her temper easily.	True	False

If you answered "False" to one or more of these questions, your teenager may not be as safe a driver as you thought. The good news is that it isn't too late to take three steps that may save his or her life—and the lives of others.

Life-Saver #1
Make sure your child makes a meaningful financial contribution to his or her driving privilege.

Kids take much better care of their cars, and drive much more carefully, when they have spent a significant amount of their own money purchasing them or paying for insurance. Using an appropriate amount of empathy, a parent might say:

- "Feel free to drive when you have enough money to pay for at least half of your own car and half of your insurance."
- "Feel free to use the family car when we don't need it and you've made a deposit into our savings account equal to the insurance deductible."

Life-Saver #2

Make it possible for your teen to drive only when you know he or she respects the rules at home and at school.

If teenagers do not respect their family or school rules, what are the chances they will respect the rules of the road? Parents need to say:

"When I know that you are ready to follow rules at home and at school, then I'll feel more comfortable that you will follow them out on the road. Then it will be time for you to drive."

Life-Saver #3

Before driving, your teen must show he/she can handle frustration without losing his/her temper.

Kids who easily lose their tempers at home are sure to lose them behind the wheel and become part of the "road rage" epidemic. With this type of child, a parent can say (without using any sarcasm):

"When I know that you handle your frustrations without throwing a fit, I will know you are ready to handle the frustrations of driving without doing something you will be sorry for later."

Love and Logic is designed to help parents raise responsible kids who are prepared to make smart choices about serious issues. Parents around the world are applying these practical strategies and finding they sleep much easier at night. You can too!

THE EVOLUTION OF THE HELICOPTER PARENT
The Turbo-Attack Helicopter Model
by Jim Fay

A joke hit the Internet recently. The problem is that it is not a joke. It's a serious concern to all those who work with today's youth.

A high school staff met to design the perfect recording for their telephone answering machine. The staff looked at several possibilities and finally agreed on the following:

To lie about why your child is absent – Press 1

To make excuses for why your child did not do his work – Press 2

To complain about what we do – Press 3

To swear at staff members – Press 4

To ask why you didn't get information that was already enclosed in your newsletter and several flyers mailed to you – Press 5

If you want us to raise your child – Press 6

If you want to reach out and touch, slap or hit someone – Press 7

To request another teacher for the third time this year – Press 8

To complain about bus transportation – Press 9

To demand that your child get a higher grade – Press 0

If you realize this is the real world and your child must be accountable/responsible for their own behavior, class and homework, and that it's not the teacher's fault for your child's lack of effort, hang up and have a great day.

I have consulted in many schools and know how overloaded teachers are today. I have witnessed the fact that teachers don't have enough spare time during the day to eat or go to the bathroom, let alone to do all the things society asks of them. This being true, why do you suppose a staff would spend its time fantasizing about this kind of thing?

Sad to say, the teachers are recognizing a national epidemic. It's the "Jet-Powered Turbo-Attack Helicopter Parent Model" epidemic. It rears its ugly head in all communities, but is especially excessive and out of control in the more affluent communities where parents have the financial resources and power to intimidate schools and community agencies.

If this is not you, just read on for the enjoyment.

Many of today's parents are obsessed with the desire to create a perfect image for their kids. This perfect image, or perfect life, is one in which their kids never have to face struggle, inconvenience, discomfort, or disappointment. It is a life in which the child can be launched into adulthood with the best of credentials. These kids look great on paper. Their high school and college diplomas show high grades even if they were not earned. They lead a life where their mistakes are swept under the table. I have often heard these parents say, "It's a competitive world out there and I want my kids to have every advantage. What they do when they are young should not hold them back later."

These parents, in their zeal to protect their young, swoop down like jet-powered, attack helicopters on any person or agency who might hold their children accountable for their actions. Armed with verbal smart bombs, they are quick to blast away at anyone who sets high standards for behavior, morality, or achievement.

Declaring their child a victim is a favorite tactical maneuver designed to send school personnel diving into the trenches for protection. Teachers and school administrators become worn down by this constant barrage. As they give in to parental demands that their children not be held accountable, standards are eroded and teachers gradually think, "What's the use?"

It is horribly disappointing to watch kids learn to blame others for their lack of success instead of becoming people who reach goals through effort and determination.

All this has caused me to look back thirty years ago to the time when we first wrote about Helicopter parents. I now realize that those parents were relatively harmless compared to the modern-day version. I daily hear about the "turbo jet-powered models" designed for deadly attack. Some of these parents are not satisfied with protection, but even prefer to destroy the infrastructure of the very agencies that are dedicated to helping their children grow into educated, moral human beings.

Now you tell me: Is it possible for children who have never had to stand on their own two feet, never had to be responsible for their own actions, or never had to face and solve the smaller problems of childhood, to have the tools to face the rigors of adult life in America? We all know the answer to that question.

Can the young adult who gets that perfect job perform well enough to keep that job if his grades from school were the result of teacher intimidation instead of vigorous study? The company who hires this person won't be easily intimidated by parental pressure in the face of substandard performance.

A perfect image and perfect school transcript are poor substitutes for character and the attitude that achievement comes through struggle and perseverance.

I have worked with many parents who have fallen into this trap. They all love their children. They all want the best for them. They talk about how they don't want their kids to struggle like they did. They are prone to rush to blame others for any lack of achievement on their child's part. These parents are willing to hold others responsible for their child's actions. However, they are often willing to change their parenting style once they see the crippling effects of this parenting style. Many of these parents have said to me, "I now realize that even if I succeed in creating a perfect life for my kid, there is little chance that they can maintain it without my help."

YOUR CHILD CAN RISE TO THE TOP

One very astute father once said to me, "Jim, I've got it. There is a huge group of trophy kids growing up today who won't have the character and resilience to compete in the labor market. If my kid grows up knowing how to get what he wants through struggle and character, he will be the one with the true advantage. He will stand head and shoulders above the others because he has the tools to create his own perfect life. Now that I have learned that I can discipline my child without losing his love, I have the courage to abandon my old crippling parenting style. The Love and Logic approach to raising my kid will give all of us the tools it takes to make this happen."

ENDING BACKTALK AND BAD ATTITUDES
Commonsense Tips for Raising Respectful Kids
by Charles Fay, Ph.D.

Parents across the country are describing the same problem: Kids who argue, role their eyes, complain, and even refuse to do what their parents ask! One mother commented, "Every time I say something to my thirteen-year-old, she gets snippy and says, 'Whatever!'"

There's good news! The following tips are time-tested and powerful:

Tip #1: When your child gets mouthy, go "brain dead."
Don't think too hard about the nasty things your kids say. The more you think, the more likely your face will turn red and the more likely you'll get sucked into a losing argument.

Tip #2: Become a loving "broken-record."
Rather than letting the arguing get to you, go "brain dead." Calmly repeat just one of the following phrases over and over regardless of what your child says:
- "I love you too much to argue."
- "I'll listen when your voice is calm like mine."
- "I know."
- "What did I say?"

Tip #3: Replace anger with empathy.
There is nothing more exciting to an argumentative, defiant child than seeing their parents' faces turn red. Pick the Love and Logic "one-liner" that works best for you. You will want to practice using it in advance to make sure that you say it with empathy, not sarcasm. Sometimes this can be hard, so practicing is important.
- "Love ya too much to argue."
- "How sad."
- "Thanks for sharing."
- "That's an option."

Tip #4: Sidestep losing power struggles by delaying consequences.
What's a parent to do if their child downright refuses to do what they ask? Don't believe the very common myth that kids always need immediate consequences. Buy yourself some time by saying:

"I'm going to do something about this—but not now, later. Try not to worry."

Tip #5: Go on strike and negotiate for better parental working conditions.
There are many extra things we do for our kids every day. Does it make sense that a healthy parent would do all of these extra things when their child is treating them like a doormat? Some parents who've decided that enough is enough quietly stop washing clothes, buying snacks, making nice meals, driving their kids to friends' houses, etc. When their kids complain, these parents calmly say:

"I love you a great deal, and I'll be happy to do the extra things I do for you when I feel treated with respect. If you aren't sure how to treat me with respect, pay close attention to how I treat you."

For over twenty-five years, parents all over this great country have changed their lives with these practical Love and Logic tips. A dad I know cured his son's acidic attitude by having a major parental power outage. Every time his son wanted something extra (like picking up a pizza, renting a video, etc.), he'd respond empathetically, "This is sad. I'll be happy to start doing those sorts of things for you when I feel treated with respect." It wasn't very long before his boy learned that being nasty just doesn't pay.

MAKE IT MOM'S DAY ALL YEAR ROUND
Teach Kids How to Treat Mom with the Respect She Deserves
by Charles Fay, Ph.D.

Mother's Day is a special day for moms to enjoy some well-deserved relaxation. An effective way for kids to help Mom on Mother's Day— and throughout the year—is by assisting with chores around the house.

Chores are an important part of family life. They provide the foundation upon which responsibility, self-esteem, and strong family relationships are built. At the Love and Logic Institute, we've found that kids who make meaningful contributions to their families, such as preparing dinner once a week or completing household chores, are more likely to succeed in school, succeed in life, and develop a desire to give back to the community.

Here are four practical, easy-to-learn tips to teach children the value of helping their mothers (and fathers) all year round:

Tip #1: Teach kids to do their fair share of the housework without being hounded.

It will make Mom's life a lot easier if kids complete chores without frequent reminders. With one simple statement, show your kids you mean business in a loving way by saying, "I'll be happy to do the things I do for you as soon as your chores are done."

Tip #2: Guide your kids toward needing less help with completing daily chores.

It's never too early to start teaching kids how to take care of themselves. As early as age two or three, kids can learn daily activities, such as getting ready in the morning, putting away toys, and preparing for bed in the evening.

In order to teach kids how to be independent, have them write down a list of daily tasks and mark them off the list as they are completed. If the child is too young to write, draw pictures of the daily tasks with your child.

Tip #3: Assign chores as repayment for withdrawals from your "emotional bank account."

When a parent asks a child to stop misbehaving, but the child keeps it up, the parent can say in a loving, soft tone of voice, "How sad! Your behavior has really drained the energy out of me. Now I'm too tired to clean the bathrooms. When you get them done, I'm sure I'll feel a whole lot better."

If the child refuses or forgets to do the chore, wise parents don't lecture or threaten. Instead, they quietly allow their child to "pay" for their bad manners with one of their favorite toys.

Tip #4: Show kids why it is wise to be polite to Mom (and Dad).
When a child talks back, pick one loving statement in response and say it over and over again, such as, "Honey, I love you too much to argue." Kids will learn that they need to use a polite tone of voice and respectful words when requesting assistance from their parents.

It's never too early or late to start raising kids to respect their parents.

I know of a mom who had to "go on strike" with her fifteen-year-old son, because he was very demanding, always wanting to know, "Where's dinner? Where are my clean clothes?" In response to her son's rude requests, she said, "I'll be happy to help you when your chores are done and I feel respected." It eased her stress level and before long, her son was a much happier, more respectful and responsible child.

NO MORE HOMEWORK BATTLES
Six Tips for Helping Kids Fall in Love with Learning
by Charles Fay, Ph.D.

Battles over reading, writing, and arithmetic too often drive a wedge between parents and their kids. Many times these ongoing conflicts give youngsters a distaste for learning and send parents to bed at night wondering, "What are we doing wrong with this kid?"

The following tips are dedicated to creating happier homes, where children are free to fall in love with learning and parents no longer dread homework hassles:

Tip #1: Each evening, set aside a time for family learning.
This is a time for your children to do their homework and for you to model the value of learning by enjoying a book. The best way to create a love of learning in your kids is to show them how much you enjoy it.

Tip #2: Avoid battles by offering choices.
Research shows children are more likely to do their homework if they are given many small choices. For example:

- "Would you rather do your homework right after school or wait until four o'clock?"
- "Are you going to do your homework in your room or at the kitchen table?"
- "Are you going to do all your homework right now or are you going to do half now and the rest after dinner?"

Tip #3: Help only when your child really wants it.

There is nothing that creates more homework battles than parents who "help" when help is not wanted. Try asking:

"Would you like some ideas on that or would you like me to leave you alone?"

Your child's desire to do it alone is a very healthy sign of independence and responsibility.

Tip #4: Spend most of your time noticing what they do well.

DO NOT focus on what your child does wrong! Allow your child to get help in those areas from their teachers. Successful parents spend 99 percent of their energy noticing what their kids do well. They say things like:

- "Show me the very best letter you made today. You really worked hard on that!"
- "Look at that math problem. You got it right!"

Tip #5: Help only as long as it's enjoyable for both of you.

Too frequently, homework help turns into a homework battle. Smart parents back out of the helper role as soon as they sense conflict brewing. Try hugging your child and saying:

"I love you too much to help if it means we are going to argue. I know this is really hard. Good luck."

Tip #6: Help only as long as your child is doing most of the work.

Say the following to yourself over and over again:

"This is my child's homework. Not mine!"

There is nothing more destructive than stealing the struggle of learning by doing too much for your child. Each time they achieve something difficult on their own, their self-esteem soars and they are better prepared for the real world.

TEACH YOUR KIDS TO HANDLE LIFE'S CONFLICTS
Why It Can Be Good for Kids to See Their Parents Disagree
by Charles Fay, Ph.D.

All relationships experience conflict. People who understand this, and know how to maintain friendships in the face of friction, enjoy a lifetime of happiness. Those who lack these skills struggle through a life filled with broken relationships and divorce. Apply the following tips, and give your kids the skills they deserve:

Tip #1: Remember that children learn the most about relationships by observing how we handle ours.
How parents handle conflicts in their marriage is typically how their children will handle conflicts in their friendships and future marriages. What we do in front of our kids is far more powerful than how we tell them to live their lives.

Tip #2: Don't make the mistake of trying to create a conflict-free family.
There's no doubt that kids suffer tremendously when they see their parents yell, argue, and fight. It's never helpful for children to witness this type of behavior.

It's also unhealthy for kids to see their parents stuff their emotions and try to pretend that nothing is wrong. This sends the unhealthy message that problems are to be avoided rather than solved.

Children are incredibly sensitive to unspoken tension. They suffer great anxiety when their parents try to hide conflicts that need to be addressed.

Tip #3: Have some healthy disagreements or conflicts in front of your kids.
Children need to see their parents disagreeing, expressing their emotions in assertive ways, and tackling conflicts head-on. It's healthy for kids to hear parents say things like, "It makes me mad when I try to

use the car and it has no gas" or "It's frustrating to me when it doesn't seem like you are listening to me."

Tip #4: Use the lingo of problem-solving and compromise.
Children also need to hear us saying things like:
- "How can we solve this problem?"
- "Let's compromise."
- "I'm sorry that I hurt your feelings."
- "Here are some possible solutions…"

Tip #5: Use common sense about what you discuss in front of your kids.
Wise parents discuss very sensitive topics only when and where their children cannot hear them.

One mother remarked, "I realize now that my husband and I were actually making it harder for our kids to have happy relationships. By trying to keep all of our disagreements a secret, we were robbing them of opportunities to see how problems can be solved. We were also creating a lot of unspoken tension that was draining the life out of our marriage."

She continued, "After following the tips you suggested, I witnessed our six-year-old arguing over a toy. I could hardly stop giggling when I heard him say, 'How can we solve this problem? Let's play something else.' That sure beats the whining contests I used to hear!"

"TEASEPROOF" YOUR KIDS
by Jim Fay

"Mom, I don't want to go to school. It's not fair. Mrs. Taylor tells the kids not to tease me, but they still do it when she's not watching 'em. I try to ignore 'em just like you said, but they just do it all the more."

Loving parents who are confronted with this feel like a piece of their heart is being ripped out. What a hopeless feeling we have when our kids are being rejected or teased by other kids. It is not uncommon at these times to have feelings that include both heartache and rage.

We think to ourselves, "Why can't the school people protect my child? Don't they realize that we put our kids in their hands, and therefore, our trust?"

The sad truth is that the more a teacher protects the child who is teased, the more resentful and aggressive the other children become. A teacher who tells kids to be nice to a specific child actually "marks" that youngster and sets them up for more intense rejection and ridicule.

When it comes to teasing, the only person who can protect your child from teasing is your child. Kids have some sort of built-in sonar that causes them to zero in on certain kids, and they can be unmerciful in the torment.

Watching this happen can be a gut-wrenching experience for any adult. But the good news is that we can actually help kids become "teaseproof."

Have you ever noticed that some kids never get teased while others are constantly subjected to teasing? There is a pattern to this.

Kids who are never teased never worry about being teased. They can't imagine that it would ever happen to them. They have an aura around them that says, "I can handle myself."

Kids who do get teased constantly worry about being ridiculed and send out nonverbal messages that indicate lack of confidence and fear of teasing. Children are especially in tune with nonverbal signals of weakness. Without realizing what they are doing they zero in on these kids. Two subconscious goals come into play. The first is, "I can show others that I am superior to that kid," and the other is, "That kid's weak and I better show him that he needs to toughen up."

Remember that none of this happens at the conscious level. It just happens and appears to be human nature.

The trick to "teaseproofing" a youngster is giving them the skills to be able to handle teasing. Once the child realizes they can actually handle the problem, you will see a change in the nonverbal attitude. The other kids will recognize this and start looking for different targets.

Mr. Mendez, a wonderful second-grade teacher, "teaseproofed" his whole class. He said to the class, "Kids, the reason kids tease other kids is that it makes them feel superior. Now you can let them get away with this or you can use an adult one-liner. But first of all, we all have to practice the 'cool look.'"

This teacher had the kids practice standing with their hands in their pockets, rocking back on their heels, and putting a cool grin on their face.

He practiced this over and over. Every now and then, he would yell out, "Let's see your 'cool look.'" The kids would all jump out of their seats and put on the "look."

Once they had all mastered the "cool look," he said, "When kids start to tease you, put on your 'cool look.' Keep the look going while they tease. As soon as they get through putting you down, use your one-liner."

The one-liner he taught them is one of the famous Love and Logic One-Liners, "Thanks for sharing that with me." Mr. Mendez had the kids practice this, making sure that they kept the "cool look" on while they said the words.

Every now and then, when the kids would least expect it, he would yell out, "Let me hear your one-liner!" And the kids would practice saying the words, making sure to grin while they said them.

Once the teacher felt that the class had mastered saying, "Thanks for sharing that with me," in the appropriate way, he started having them practice jumping up out of their seats, putting on the "cool look," and saying their one-liner.

The next step was for the kids to learn to turn around on the last word and walk away fast without looking back at the teasing child. Needless to say, they all did their practice until the skill was mastered. They even spent some of their recess time practicing this on the playground.

Now that the skill had been learned, practiced, and mastered, Mr. Mendez could implement his part of the operation. When children came to him to tattle about others teasing them, he consistently asked, "Did you let him get by with it or did you use your 'cool skill'?"

In the event that the child admitted that he had not used their skill, the teacher said, "How sad that you let him get away with it. Do you suppose you are going to continue to let him get by with it or are you going to use your skill? It's your choice, but tattling to me is no longer a choice."

Mr. Mendez tells us that the amount of tattling and complaining has been reduced by over 90%. He also proudly tells about one of his students who came to him asking if they had to use the one-liner he taught them, or could make up their own.

This second-grader wanted to demonstrate to the class the one-liner that he used so successfully on the playground.

He stood before the class and said, "This other kid on the playground was dissin' me. He said I had the skinniest arms in the whole school. I put on my 'cool look.' I grinned and said, 'Bummer, I thought I was cool, man.' I walked away before he could figure out what to say. Man, I blew his mind!"

All the kids clapped for this skillful second-grader, and the teacher beamed with pride as he thought to himself, "Now that kid is really 'teaseproofed' for sure."

You don't have to wait for the teacher to "teaseproof" your kids. You can do it in your home the same way Mr. Mendez did in the classroom. What a gift you can give your child, and come to think of it, what a gift it is to a parent to know that we can send our kids out into the world "teaseproofed."

Since the development of the "cool look" skill, many different kids have found sanctuary in its use. One of the most creative applications was seen at a local school where the kids seem to take great pleasure in claiming to do research on the behavior of other kids' mothers and attacking each other with this information when they are mad.

One kid yelled out to the other, "Yo momma's a ho." The youngster being attacked put on his "cool look" and replied, "I tell her to be nice, but she gets mad when I tell her what to do." With this he turned and walked away.

The teacher who witnessed this reported that the attacker's mouth fell open and all he could say under his breath was, "Man, that guy's weird. He be weird."

Now the kid who pulled this one off is absolutely "teaseproofed." Even if kids try to tease him, the attacks will bounce off like Ping-Pong balls off a stone wall.

THE IMPORTANCE OF CHORES
by Charles Fay, Ph.D.

Chores are an important part of a child's life. They provide the foundation upon which responsibility and high self-esteem are built. Chores need not—indeed should not be—a cause of parent/child friction.

Guideline 1: When children are small, enjoy doing things together.

When children are small they like to "copy" and "model" their parents. When they are small they say, "Let me do it. " (Oh, wouldn't it be a joy if they said that at ten!) Little ones like to stir around in the dishwater as the parent does the dishes. They like to dress up just like their parents. They like to push around their Fisher-Price lawn mower as if really cutting the grass. So, during the toddler years, it is the wise parent who communicates the following messages:

- "Hey, I like getting my job done around the house.
  It's fun for me!"
- "Wow, I enjoy doing things with you!"
- "Don't we have fun together?"

Guideline 2: Base chores on the maturity of your child.

I say "maturity" because maturity level may not always reflect the child's actual age. Generally, however, through kindergarten, the child is of no real help with most tasks. During the preschool and kindergarten years, the correct attitude about chores is built mainly by parents modeling and "working" with the child. Preschool and kindergarten children may be expected to clean up messes they make, help clean up their rooms, and make their beds (even if only in a sloppy sort of way).

By third grade and throughout the rest of the elementary school years, most children can take care of the dishes and clean a few of the family rooms once a week. Other jobs they can handle include cleaning the garage, cleaning the car (inside and out), taking out the trash, and cleaning dirty windows.

Guideline 3: The secret to making chores a happy experience for your child is to use consequences without anger.

Children do not need to be rewarded for finishing a job. However, compliments and happiness are important. All of us like to hear more excitement about things done right than things done wrong! All of us need positive comments and interactions with others. If parents convey more emotion about jobs done poorly than jobs done well, you can bet jobs will continue to be done poorly.

I do not recommend tying allowance to chores. This is not the way the real world works. Parents don't get paid for fixing dinner or going shopping. It's expected as part of their contribution to the family unit.

The rub comes in applying appropriate consequences, without anger, when jobs have been done poorly or have not been completed. Let's look at this example:

A new parent, trying to be a good parent, once asked a mother why she was able to do a better job of raising eight children than most people did with one. The mother thought for a while and finally said, "Well, I really don't know. All I can say is, if the eggs aren't gathered, nobody has breakfast."

That's it! How simple. It's just like the real world. First do your job, and then you can eat! This young parent used the idea. As her children grew into adulthood, she always let them know that she would like the job done by the time they ate their next meal. They could take their time. No rush. But she found the job was always done by dinnertime.

Chores are the foundation of responsibility and self-esteem.

I hope that as you've read the stories in this book, you've learned some techniques that will make your life, and the life of your kids, easier, less stressful, and a lot more fun. There's no greater gift we can give our kids than the gift of responsibility and good character. Thanks for reading!

Accountability, 35, 37, 62
  importance of, 63
  limits and, 1-2
  poor decisions and, 3, 57
  problem solving and, 4
Achievement, 63, 64
Acting out, 5
Adult-child relationships, 23
Alcohol, 9
Allowances, 6, 7, 14
  arguing over, 12
  chores and, 76
Anger, 22, 43, 57, 58
  breaking cycle of, 24
  consequences and, 76
  dignity and, 29
  empathy and, 45-46, 65
  limits and, 2, 4
  showing, 12, 23
  worrying and, 29
Anti-argue skills, 13, 31-32
Arguing, 12, 16, 23, 35, 37, 65, 69, 70
  ending, 19, 32
  successful, 17
Arithmetic
  battles over, 68
  building blocks for, 56
Attitudes, 15
  bad, ending, 65-66
Authority figures, 57, 58

Baby-sitting, paying for, 17, 22
Battles
  encouraging, 5, 6
  homework, 68-70
Bedtime, preparations at, 67
Begging, 24, 25

Behavior
  concerns about, 33-34
  criminal, 34, 35
  modeling, 2
  problems with, 37, 56
  responsibility for, 62
  standards for, 63
  See also Misbehavior
Blaming, 37, 44, 45, 63, 64
Brain, 43
  connections, 57
  function of, 41, 42
  growing, 57
Brain dead, 12-13, 16, 65
Brain stem, 42, 43
  "fight or flight" response and, 41
"Brain switch," 41
Broken-record, 16, 65
"Bummer," 15, 23, 31, 35, 44, 46, 47,
    52, 74
Buttons, pushing, 11

Character
  creating, 33, 34, 36, 37, 38, 39
  gift of, 76
  lack of, 64
Choices, 59, 61
  offering, 52, 68-69
Chores, 8, 13, 23
  allowances and, 76
  completing, 67, 68
  helping with, 66-67
  importance of, 75-76
  responsibility and, 66-67
Cline, Foster W., 51, 55
Compassion, 15, 35
Complaining, 62, 65, 73-74

Compliments, importance of, 76
Compromise, language of, 71
Confidence, teasing and, 72
Conflicts, handling, 70-71
Consequences
  anger and, 76
  anticipatory, 32
  decision making and, 22, 50
  delaying, 66
  delivering, 4, 22-23, 27, 30
  empathy and, 45
  experiencing, 38, 39
  immediate, 27-29, 66
  logical, 27-28, 32
  meaningful, 31, 58
  problems with, 28-29
  punishment and, 35
  thinking/planning and, 28
Consultant parents, 39, 62
  described, 38
Control, losing, 16
Cool look, teasing and, 72-73, 74
Creativity, 57
Criticism, 43
Curfews, 31

Decision making
  accountability for, 3, 34, 35, 57
  good, x, xi, 38
  learning from, 34
  poor, 22, 50
Defensive mode, 41
Dependency, 38
Dignity, 29
Directions, following, 56
Disagreements, healthy, 70-71
Disappointment, 63
Discipline, 37, 46
  love/respect and, xi, 64
Discomfort, 63
Disrespect, 56
Divorce, 70

"Dr. Laura" show, listening to, 33
Drill sergeants, xi, 39
  described, 38
Driving privilege, ix, 60-61

Embarrassment, 24, 43, 56
Emotional bank accounts, chores
  and, 67
Empathy
  anger and, 45-46, 65
  consequences and, 45
  dignity and, 29
  learning and, 31
  locking in, 4, 22-23, 24, 27, 28, 30,
    35, 37
  power of, 39, 47
  providing, 41, 43, 45, 53, 60
Employers, respect for, 58
"Ending Backtalk and Bad Attitudes:
  Commonsense Tips for Raising
  Respectful Kids" (Fay), 65-66
Energy, 16, 24
  draining, 58, 59, 67
Enforceable statements, 7, 12, 16, 19
  examples of, 9
  fighting words vs., 8
Everyday activities, talking
  about, 57
"Evolution of the Helicopter Parent:
  The Turbo-Attack Helicopter
  Model, The" (Fay), 61-64
Examples, setting, 7
Excuses, 29, 35, 37, 62
Expectations, high, 57
Experiments, 32, 47, 58-59

Family
  conflict-free, 70
  focusing on, x-xi
Fay, Charles, ix, x, xi
  article by, 55-59, 65-66, 66-67, 68-70,
    70-71, 75-76

Fay, Jim, ix, x-xi, 14, 55
  article by, 61-64, 71-74
  lesson for, 49-50
Fay, Shirley, 49-50, 51, 53
Fighting, 6, 7, 43-44, 70
Fighting words
  enforceable statements vs., 8
  thinking words vs., 6
"Fight or flight" response, 41, 42, 45
Four Steps to Responsibility (Fay), ix
Friendships, maintaining, 70
Frontal cortex, using, 41, 42-43, 46
Frustration, 12, 24, 37, 58
  dealing with, 41-42, 60, 61

Getting ready to go, 19-20, 67
Guidance, 38
Guilt, 35

Happiness, 76
Helicopter parents, 39, 61-64
  described, 38
Holding the line, 35-36
Homework, 8, 14
  battles over, 68-70
  choices about, 68-69
"How sad," 46, 65, 67, 73

"I know," 17, 24, 30, 31, 65
  using, 12-13, 14, 15
"Importance of Chores, The" (Fay),
  75-76
Inconvenience, 63
Independence, 69
Ineffective statements, 7, 8
Insurance, 60, 61
Interruptions, avoiding, 56
"I will" statements, 7
  "You will" statements vs., 8

"Keep Teenagers Safe Behind the
Wheel: Practical Tips for Parents

Who Want to Be Sure" (Fay), 60-61
Kid attack, vulnerability to, 24
Kindness, 57

Learning
  consequences and, 31
  empathy and, 31
  falling in love with, 68-70
  opportunities for, 22, 34, 35, 71
  stealing, 38
  struggling with, 69-70
  successful, 55
Lectures, 23, 39, 67
  avoiding, 16, 37
  limits and, 2, 4
Libraries, visiting, 57
Limits
  enforcing, 24
  setting, 1, 2, 4-7, 11, 12, 19, 24, 37, 58
  testing, 1-2, 5, 12
  thinking words and, 6
Listening, 9, 56, 58-59
Love
  discipline and, xi, 64
  feeling, 57
  increasing, 3
  losing, 2
Love and Logic, 19, 30, 31
  consequences and, 32
  learning, x, 1
Love and Logic Institute, 7, 67
Love and Logic Journal, 55
Lying, 34, 62

Mabel, the babysitter from hell,
  21-22, 24
"Make It Mom's Day All Year Round:
  Teach Kids How to Treat Mom with
  the Respect She Deserves" (Fay),
  66-67
Manipulation, 12, 13-14, 15-16, 37
Marriages, conflicts in, 70

Misbehavior, 24, 34
  consequences for, 17, 22, 28
  empathy for, 23
  handling, 36, 58
  limits and, 5
  See also Behavior
Mistakes, xi, 63
Modeling, 2, 7, 23, 75
Morality, 63
Mother's Day, 66-67

Nagging, 4, 50
National Highway and Transportation
    Safety Administration, 60
Neighbors, 20, 21, 24, 30
Neurological pathways, 57
"Nice try," 14, 15, 24, 31
No big deal, 33
"No More Homework Battles:
    Six Tips for Helping Kids Fall in
    Love with Learning" (Fay), 68-70

One-liners, 12-16, 65
  teasing and, 72-73, 74
Orders, avoiding, 5, 6

Pain, owning, 22
Parental working conditions, 66
Parent-child confidentiality, 34
Parenting, ix, 59
  fun/rewarding, 17, 57
Parents
  respect for, 66-67, 68
  types of, 38-39, 61-64
Patience, 58
Paying attention, 56
Perseverance, achievement and, 64
Picking fights, 6, 7
Playing, 57
Police officers, children and, 57
Politeness, importance of, 56, 67
Power struggles, 4, 37, 66

Principals, types of, 43-45
Problems, handing back, 3, 4, 27, 28, 36
Problem solving, 3, 23, 37, 38
  accountability and, 4
  language of, 71
Punishment, 35, 45

Reading, 57
  battles over, 68
  building blocks for, 56
Real world, preparing for, 38, 62, 70, 76
Reasoning, building blocks for, 56
Rehearsal, 24, 29, 30
Rejection, 71, 72
Relationships, learning about, 70
Reminders, 49, 50, 67
Remorse, 44
Rescuing, 37, 38, 39
Resentment, 22
Resilience, lack of, 64
Resistance, creating, 6
Respect, xi, 53
  increasing, 3
  losing, 2
  treating with, 6, 66-67, 68
Responsibility, 34, 35, 62
  avoiding, 63
  chores and, 66-67, 75, 76
  entitlement and, xi
  gift of, 76
  learning, 2, 22, 69
  taking, 45
  teaching, x, 25, 50, 61
Revenge, 23, 43, 44, 45
"Road rage," 61
Rocky Mountain Conference, 13-14
Rolling eyes, 11, 65
Rules, following, 60, 61

Sadness, sincere, 46
Safe, feeling, 57
Sarcasm, avoiding, 13, 65